Praise for *Freedom*

Very rarely does one encounter the
toral insight, cultural engagement, theological sharpness, and exegetical talent displayed in this fine book. It is wise, reflects years of teaching and pastoral experience, and will be a joy to read for pastors, teachers, and the more general culture.

—Christopher Seitz, senior research professor of biblical interpretation, Wycliffe College in the University of Toronto

It has been said that the crisis of modernity is a failure of trust. In this lucid and stimulating study, Giere goes much deeper than this, showing that the root issue is the absence of the kind of trust God makes possible in Jesus.

—Jeremy Begbie, professor of theology, Duke University

S. D. Giere teaches that the gospel of Jesus Christ is ontologically relevant and that our call as Christian preachers and teachers is to avoid rendering the gospel irrelevant. In this biblically grounded, honest, and holy exploration of what he describes as the freedom and imagination of faith, S. D. Giere illustrates just how relevant the gospel of Jesus Christ is to how we live and breathe today. I highly recommend this book to all faith leaders and explorers alike.

—Rev. Leila M. Ortiz, bishop of the Metropolitan Washington, D.C. Synod of the ELCA

Freedom and Imagination offers a timely and wide-ranging study of the Christian life as trust in Jesus Christ, contrasting that life with trust in the false gods dominating the cultural and political landscape of our day, whether on the right or on the left. It tells the story of how the "bad faith" produced by our misdirected trust in "ideology" displaces Jesus Christ, the eternal and risen Lord, from the center of the gospel, replacing the gospel with "broken cisterns" (Jer 2:13) unequal to the task of reconciling the world to God in Christ. This book challenges the church of our day to embrace a cross-shaped and reconciled imagination that exists apart from our ideologies. While I was reading it, a lyric from Bruce Cockburn's "Child of the Wind" came to mind: "Little round planet in a big universe, sometimes it looks blessed, sometimes it looks cursed. Depends on what you look at, obviously. But even more it depends on the way that you see." Giere's book will reorient the way that you see (fair warning to potential readers!).

—Don Collett, professor of Old Testament, Trinity Episcopal School of Ministry, and author of *Figural Reading and the Old Testament: Theology and Practice*

FREEDOM AND IMAGINATION

FREEDOM & IMAGINATION

Trusting Christ in an Age of Bad Faith

S. D. Giere

FORTRESS PRESS
MINNEAPOLIS

FREEDOM AND IMAGINATION
Trusting Christ in an Age of Bad Faith

Cover design and illustration: Brice Hemmer

Print ISBN: 978-1-5064-8235-4
eBook ISBN: 978-1-5064-8236-1

To the Dubuque Fire Pipes and Drums and the regulars at Monk's Kaffee Pub and the Bier Stube, motley crews all

Contents

Preface

So there I was . . .

When I started chatting with friends about the idea for this book, there was interest and a host of ideas. A few good ideas, many terrible ones, mostly unsolicited, but often good fun! A suggestion that has persisted is that "a great opening line" for the book would be, *So, no shit, there I was . . .* After thinking about this proposition for some months now, it is fitting, as the ideas that play out in this book have germinated as much outside the formal bounds of the church and theological education as in, sprouting largely in accidental communities, motley crews of sincere folks carrying a wide range of existential concerns, religious ideas, and experiences of the church.

While working on this book, the proverbial "choir" that is regularly preached to has not been at the front of my mind. Rather, it has been these accidental communities. Groups of friends and strangers who fall into community and conversation about what matters in their lives, whose questions and selves the church has often found objectionable. These accidental communities that I count as my own are often a hodgepodge of folks with strong beliefs and opinions, some right leaning, others left leaning. For some, the very idea of purple is anathema; others couldn't give a hoot. And yet often over a coffee or a pint, community happens, relationships germinate, and conversations from substantive to small break out.

For better or worse, I have told students for years that it is not their job to make the gospel relevant, as the gospel of Jesus Christ is ontologically relevant because it has to do with death and life, with meaning, with beauty. Rather than making the gospel relevant, the challenge before them as ministers of the gospel of Jesus Christ is to avoid rendering that gospel irrelevant.

What plays out on the following pages is an attempt to poke at a challenge that faces the church today—What is the center of this whole thing and why care? What is the core relevancy of the gospel, which so many people have experienced as irrelevant or worse? Truth be told, there are a few billion people on the planet who live their lives just fine without a need for the church. So why does this whole churchy Christian business matter? Alongside this, what is appealing or persuasive about the gospel of Jesus Christ, especially for those not already Christian or those formerly Christian?

Pondering these questions in recent years, I've been drawn regularly to a problem (perhaps the primary problem): we, the church, wittingly and unwittingly displace the gospel with any number of ideologies and thereby replace Jesus as Lord and Savior with ourselves. Sure, this is harsh language and a sweeping judgment. I do hope that what follows both agitates and offers a hopeful suggestion or two.

In 2 Corinthians, Paul writes, "From now on, therefore, we regard no one from a human point of view; even though we once regarded Christ from a human point of view, we regard him thus no longer. Therefore, if any one is in Christ, he is a new creation; the old has passed away, behold, the new has come" (2 Cor 5:16–17 RSV). New creation in Christ is a critical intersection of freedom, faith, imagination. Christ, the one who makes free (John 8:36), invites the individual to participate in this freedom through faith (trust; Rom 5:10). Faith, which is participation in Christ, invites us to see ourselves and the world around us, our neighbor and our enemy, the whole of creation in the light of new creation. Notwithstanding the promise of new creation, the world looks a mess. We look a mess. Frankly, the church often looks a mess. This dissonance between what faith invites us to see as reality, a cosmos that God has reconciled to God's self through the cross of Christ—that is, new creation—and what we see and experience day-to-day can be significant, even jarring. Good, noble-minded Christians, both right and left, get fed up with the dissonance and try to do what God alone is capable of. As such, we try to take the reins (and reign!) from God in the interest of fixing the world ourselves. The obvious unrighteousness within and around us begs for correction. In the interest of some proper and timely fecal coordination (that is, getting our shit together), faith in Jesus devolves into trusting in oneself or in an ideology, both of which make promises that they/we cannot keep. In this "bad faith," we miss the vital role of imagination, reconciled in and through trusting in Jesus. Participating in the new creation, which is completely and fully God's doing, we are invited to see the world in and through Christ, guided perhaps by Jesus's prayer from the cross: "Father, forgive them; for they know not what they do" (Luke 23:24 RSV). While there might be glimpses of the new creation from time to time, it is something primarily witnessed and understood in and through trust in Jesus Christ.

This argument, which takes seriously the centrality of faith and the corporeal, incarnational reality of imagination, moves toward a freedom in Christ.

There are so many pressing issues before the world today, some ancient and some new. The human capacity for violence remains amazingly persistent. We can maim and kill one another with cold efficiency. We have gotten quite proficient in recent centuries with genocide and the rhetoric that leads people to distrust and hate one another. In the name of progress, we humans have placed the habitability of large swaths of the planet in jeopardy, with a disproportionate impact on poorer people and nations. The arrogance of colonial righteousness has forcibly divorced many humans and communities from their value, heritage, and belonging. The argument of this book, that the imagination of faith in Jesus Christ is the Christian's way of envisioning freedom in Christ, is *not* a pie-in-the-sky attempt to turn us from reality. Rather, the freedom that comes in Christ opens the world for engagement with these challenges without the notion that the church or the Christian has some sort of corner on the market for how things should be. The freedom that accompanies the imagination of faith opens the person to converse, work, live with any and everyone: theists and atheists, skeptics, cynics, the pious, folks of all cultures and religions. (Practically speaking, you still need to be mindful of jerks. While no less children of God, they are a challenge to mental health.)

A hundred years ago, Swiss theologian Karl Barth revised his commentary on Paul's Epistle to the Romans against the tumultuous backdrop of the end of World War I. Commenting on Romans 5:1–11, he writes, "By faith we attain the status of those who have been declared righteous before God. *By faith we are what we are not.*"[1]

Trusting in Jesus, which is faith, by the power of the Spirit creates that which is not. That is, by faith, God makes the sinner, the one out of whack, righteous. Given that all are sinners and fall short of the glory of God (Rom 3:23b–25a), there is a level field whereupon faith opens vistas upon the world as it is in Christ. Barth is right that by faith, we are what we are not, but it goes further. By faith, the world is revealed as it is in Christ. This is new creation. This is freedom.

So there I was, pondering faith, imagination, and freedom, hoping to start a conversation. In faith—that is, trusting in Jesus—there is a beauty that longs to be shared, especially for those who have experienced the church's judgment or disinterest.

Wartburg Theological Seminary
September 1, 2022

1 Barth, *Epistle to the Romans*, 149.

Acknowledgments

This little book is the result of many points of intersection over the past decade and would not have materialized if not for the support of many.

After completing a PhD in Old Testament at the University of St. Andrews, I started teaching homiletics at Wartburg Theological Seminary in Dubuque, Iowa. While not what I had envisioned for a teaching career, I felt the call to give it a go. After fifteen years of stewarding the formation of preachers, I can say that I learned a great deal and might have even had an impact on some students and by extension congregations near and far. My biblical work up to the point of taking the homiletics gig had been a strange mix of philology, history of interpretation, and hermeneutics. The shift in vocational focus opened the way for me over time to reconfigure my theological hermeneutic from an uneasy marriage of postmodernity and historical-critical methods to one focused on the theological questions and claims of the biblical text within a long and variegated history of interpretation. The students that I have had the pleasure (at least most of the time) to accompany in their formation as interpreters and preachers have formed me as a biblical scholar and theologian. In many ways, the theological curriculum is laid bare, butt naked before the world, when someone gets up to preach. There is a necessary integration of biblical study, church history, theology, ethics, leadership, pastoral care, and so on that coalesce in the art of preaching as someone dares to proclaim the living Word aloud to the world *in such a way that this Word can be heard as good news for that time and place.* My time with students as they simultaneously grabbed hold of and received this dare has in turn formed my thinking and my imagination about the imagination of faith. To you, dear students, I am grateful.

To the institution that has supported my teaching and scholarship, Wartburg Theological Seminary, and to my faculty colleagues, to leadership and staff, and to our board of directors for their continued support of a generous sabbatical policy, I am grateful.

When I think of individuals who have played a role, some without knowing it, in the coalescing of these ideas, the first to come to mind is Professor Duane A. Priebe, who served for fifty years as professor of systematic theology and for a number of years as academic dean at Wartburg. Duane, now bearing the weight of dementia, was my teacher, colleague, and confidant. When I returned to Wartburg to teach, he invited me to help facilitate a long-standing weekly Wartburg tradition: beer and theology. B&T, as it is affectionately known, was and remains an informal time for students, faculty, guests, and friends to gather for a pint and theological reflection. There are many of his ideas woven throughout this book, likely more than I am aware of. With Duane's retirement, I have continued the tradition of B&T in partnership with friend and former student Jennifer Agee, a poet and a keen theologian with a deep appreciation for a Christocentric imagination and for the place of bees in our life together on the planet. With her accompaniment, I have grown in my thinking and appreciation for the Inklings and for the imagination's role in theology, art, and science.

I would also like to express gratitude to the following individuals for conversation and support in and around these topics in recent years: Louise Johnson; Kirstin Jeffrey Johnson; Pete Morrison, the bard of South Bowhill; Paul Wallace; Carmelo Santos; Don Collett; Gunnar Sigurjónsson; Þóra Þórarinsdóttir; Arnfriður Guðmundsdóttir; Gunnar Runár Mathíasson; Guðný Hallgrímsdóttir; Øystein Aronsen; Sunniva Gylver; Lars Gylver; Shadoe Hanson; Marie Martinez; Jake Kurczek; Dicky Goodrich; Trish Feldman-Jansen; Kasey Jansen; Randy Nichols; Paul Jelinek; Dale Russell; Jackie Baumhover; Lily Reed; Matthew O'Rear; Patrick Conlon;

Cathy Conlon; Winston Dwarka Persaud; May Burt Persaud; Neely Farren-Eller, Eric Eller, Rachel Dilling, and Rachel Daack of the "I'm a Dubuquer" campaign;[2] and bandmates in the Dubuque Fire Pipes and Drums (DBQFPD), in particular Bill Grant, Bill Spivey, Joe Berger, Dave Hawkins, and Kevan Blindheim Norin. To this motley crew, cheers!

I have had the pleasure of presenting earlier versions of these ideas at the Luther Academy of the Rockies, with clergy of the Evangelical Lutheran Church in Iceland, and at the Southeastern, South Dakota, Southwestern Minnesota, and LaCrosse Area Synods of the Evangelical Lutheran Church in America. The collegial questions, feedback, and pushback have proved both energizing and helpful.

I have always appreciated the work of editors. Editing is often a thankless, behind-the-scenes slog. Not that this book has been a slog (!), but I do want to express my gratitude to Ryan Hemmer for his editorial work and for shepherding the project and also to Fortress Press for their willingness to see the project through.

To my dear spouse and partner in this wild life, Amy Current, herself an excellent preacher and a wise theologian, for being a constant source of encouragement, insight, and support, thank you. As I am one who tends to hang out somewhere between skepticism and cynicism with regard to the institutional church, she reminds me regularly of the good and hopeful aspects of the church that exist and thrive and that don't give a hoot about my jaded perspective. This is a true gift. Our offspring, Isaac and Shonagh, have been supportive and willing to listen to me prattle on about the project. You three have my gratitude and love.

There are geniuses and savants on the planet. I have met a few. Some friends even qualify. I do not. Likewise, there are poets and authors and artists who help us see and hear and feel the world

2 For a bit of background on this project that worked to broaden people's imaginations about our local community in Dubuque, Iowa, see Beason, "Nearly All-White." A video spot hosted by reporter Tyrone Beason on race in Dubuque included a reference to the campaign, with an evening dinner chat in our family's home: https://youtu.be/HDGY6auD9xc.

differently—sometimes more clearly, sometimes assisting others in envisioning the world as it could or might be. And likewise, I am not one. I am a photography enthusiast, an amateur bagpiper, and a scholar greatly appreciative of being able to spend some time and share some thoughts in the intersectional space that the imagination of faith occupies.

I am convinced that trusting in Jesus matters, as it opens and reveals the world as one worthy of wonder and sometimes even joy—a world that Christ, by his incarnation, death, resurrection, and ascension, has taken into the very heart of God, a world that receives love because of who God is, not because of what we do or who we are. The motley crews at Monk's, the Bier Stube, and the Dubuque Fire Pipes and Drums have provided space for considering the imagination of faith and the freedom that accompanies it, and they have helped keep my feet on the ground. For this, I am grateful, and I dedicate this little book to them.

CHAPTER ONE

An Age of Bad Faith

> Be appalled, O heavens, at this, be shocked, be utterly desolate, says the Lord, for my people have committed two evils: they have forsaken me, the fountain of living waters, and hewed out cisterns for themselves, broken cisterns, that can hold no water.
>
> —Jeremiah 2:12–13 (RSV)

Picture a wooden building. This wooden building stands tall and looks pretty good. It's not perfect. It shows the wear and tear of weather and use and time. But it has a fresh coat of paint and new windows, and its shingles are in good enough shape. A problem at the center of the structure, however, lurks unseen. The girder of this wooden building, the primary load-bearing beam that is key to holding the whole structure up and together, suffers from dry rot. It is riddled with decay that is not easy to see. Dry rot puts the whole building in peril.

The church in North America has its own dry rot. It too is in unseen peril. From the outside, it looks OK. But serious dry rot at the biblical and theological core places the sturdiness of the whole in jeopardy.[1] I am calling this dry rot an "age of bad faith." To use

---

1 The metaphor of dry rot is borrowed from Brevard S. Childs, who offered a critique of and way forward for biblical study with his 1979 book *An Introduction to the Old Testament as Scripture*, published through Fortress Press. Childs's concern was the developing chasm between the academic study of the Bible and

such language might well sound ominous. Even gloomy. Well, it is meant to.

This book attempts to open a conversation about these unseen problems. It offers a means of thinking about the health of the structure by looking carefully and creatively at the center girder of Christianity: faith in Jesus Christ. Faith, which is trusting in Jesus Christ, invites the Christian into the world as it has been reconciled by God in Christ, a world that is accessible to us through the reconciled imagination.

There are several aspects of being a Lutheran that I quite appreciate (and a few that I don't). One that I most value is Martin Luther's assertion that being a theologian of the cross means "calling a thing what it actually is."[2] To translate the promise of Christ crucified for one's day, time, and place means turning full-on toward the situation of the church and the world and describing it in language that people can understand. This chapter is an attempt to do just that. The bulk of the rest of the book turns toward the hope that is trusting Jesus Christ—the Christian's and the church's means of structural integrity.

---

the place of the Bible in the life of faith, the result of which was that "something was fundamentally wrong with the foundations of the biblical discipline" (15). His assessment was that this problem had to do with the interpreter's concept of the Bible. Just what is Christian Scripture? His proposal, rooted in a theology of revelation, would become a canonical approach, an attempt to see not just a collection of disparate pieces but a whole.

2 Heidelberg Disputation (1518), in *LW* 31.39. I credit my dear spouse for offering a critique of my original metaphor for the current situation as a "shit-mess." In the interest of offending you, my dear reader, as properly as possible, I received her critique of my vulgarity and shifted to *dry rot*, which I am confident helps get at the seriousness of the matter. At the same time, and in the spirit of imagination and being a theologian of the cross, it is worth pondering George Carlin's bit "Seven Words You Can't Say on TV," from the early 1970s; YouTube video, https://youtu.be/8dCIKqkIg1w.

BAD FAITH AND THE THIN LINE BETWEEN FAITH AND SIN

The line between faith and sin is razor-thin. Both share the same core dynamic: trust. The difference between the two is in the object of that trust. Sin is trusting in that which is not the triune God, while faith is trusting in the triune God. In sixteenth-century Germany, an Augustinian friar named Martin Luther struggled to make sense of who God was and, in particular, how human beings were to relate to God. He fretted about how an imperfect human being such as himself should relate to the Almighty, who is perfect and demands perfection.[3] Through a good deal of emotional and intellectual wrestling, he had a series of theological lightbulbs turn on. His primary insight pertained to how imperfect human beings relate to Almighty God. His answer was simple: faith.

To get at that simplicity, we need to have a quick polka with the Greek word that in the Bible is often translated as "faith": *πίστις* (*pistis*). Liddell and Scott, authors of the standard-bearer lexicon for all ancient Greek literature, note that the word that the church knows as *faith* is at its root "trust."[4] It is a relationship, not an object. Trust is something that we participate in even before we are born. Our first experience of trust comes in and from the womb, wherein we rely completely upon our mother for the whole of our well-being until we emerge into the world. Central to this emergence is the intimate relationship of trust with our mother and the world to which she first introduces us.

Often the word *faith* is accompanied by churchy baggage. Some of that baggage is good. Some, not so much. But I am guessing that it is rare to hear the word *faith* and begin reminiscing about the comfort and security of the womb. We will return to explore faith as trust in more depth in chapter 2. For the moment, remember that faith at its core is trust.

---

3 "Be perfect, therefore, as your heavenly Father is perfect" (Matt 5:48).

4 Liddell and Scott, *Greek-English Lexicon*.

The thin line between faith and sin, then, is the object of trust—that is, *that in which we trust*. The object of faith is the triune God (e.g., Eph 2:8), whom the Christian is called to trust for life, healing, wholeness, and salvation. The object of trust that is sin is quite literally anything else. Yes, it is that simple. Seeking life, healing, wholeness, and salvation from anything or anyone else is sin.

In his explanation of the first commandment in his *Large Catechism* (1529), Luther gets to the heart of the matter of this similarity of faith and sin. Recall that the Lord says, "You shall have no other gods before me" (Exod 20:3 RSV).[5] Rather than limit "other gods" to mere material things like a golden calf, Luther orients "other gods" around trust: "Anything on which your heart relies and depends, I say, that is really your God."[6] To put it just a bit differently, that in which you place your trust is your god. In essence, sin is idolatry, which is trusting in that which is not God. Faith, on the other hand, is trusting in the triune God. This difference is a thin but crucial line.

Consider this thin line in straightforward terms: the difference is between good faith and bad faith. Good faith is trust in Jesus Christ—entrusting oneself, one's life, one's healing, one's wholeness, one's community, the living and the dead, and ultimately, the cosmos to the living God. Bad faith is trusting in anything else for life, for healing, for wholeness.

As the Lord says in Jeremiah's poetic way, "They have forsaken me, the fountain of living waters, and hewed out cisterns for themselves, broken cisterns, that can hold no water" (Jer 2:13 RSV). Bad faith is more akin to a sieve than a cistern. To say that we are in an age of bad faith (an age of homemade, broken cisterns, while accurate, does not have the same punch) is a claim about the object of our

5 The *Large Catechism* was designed by Luther to be a guide for preachers and for teachers of the *Small Catechism*. Luther was convinced that the church benefits when both clergy and laity are educated. They are both structured in a way that interweaves piety and learning, as the organizing principles are the Ten Commandments, the Apostles' Creed, and the Lord's Prayer, with additional instruction on the sacraments, prayer, and other aspects of day-to-day piety. See Kolb and Wengert, *Book of Concord*, 345–480.

6 *BC* 386.3.

faith—whether as a collective or as individuals. We trust other gods. And like Jon Bon Jovi (almost) says in his hair-metal anthem, bad faith, like bad medicine, "can't cure my disease."[7] We are living in an age of bad faith that does not have the capacity to cure our disease, which is a sin/idolatry that results in an imagination enslaved to fear and death.

We worship that in which we put our trust. Paul Tillich's (1886–1965) language of "ultimate concern" is helpful here, as it puts another gloss on Luther's point: that in which you put your trust is your god. What is our ultimate concern? What is *your* ultimate concern? What do you worship? While the worship of power, wealth, death, and culture remain steadfast in our catalog of "golden calves," in recent decades, we can add ideology to the list. Righteousness (i.e., being right and/or just, whether in the eyes of the church or society) is predominantly measured in terms of trust and worship of these gods. We worship these gods, wittingly or unwittingly, because they demand our allegiance, our sacrifice. They beg for our trust by promising that which they cannot deliver: life. In so doing, they hold us captive. A primary means of this captivity is the limitation and/or misdirection of our imagination, inviting us to imagine the world as something other than a cosmos reconciled to the triune God by the death and resurrection of Jesus Christ. The result is a disimagination of ourselves and the world around us.

Faith/trust in Jesus Christ is the center of Christian life. When the center that bears the load for the whole structure begins to deteriorate, whether it's faith or the sinus rhythm of your heart, the whole system gets sick and can begin to collapse. It is dry rot. When Jesus Christ—the eternal, incarnate, crucified, and risen Word—is displaced as Lord and Savior, as the object of our trust, there is a domino effect throughout the whole. Theology is reduced to anthropology. The mystery of faith is reduced to ethics.

A big claim? Yes.

7 "Bad Medicine," MP3 audio, track 2 on Bon Jovi, *New Jersey*, Mercury, 1988.

I have spent the last fifteen years stewarding the formation of preachers. During this time, I quit keeping track of the number of sermons that I heard. I joke with tongue in cheek that I secretly hope there is a purgatory, as I've earned myself some get-out-of-purgatory-free cards over the years.[8] This is no disrespect to my students or to my faculty colleagues who share responsibility for their formation or to other preachers who have participated in the formation of these students, especially prior to answering the call to ministry and attending seminary. We are all doing the best we can. And yet there is a clear and persistent thread in the preaching that I have heard in the classroom and in churches wherein Jesus is displaced as the object of trust and replaced not by a golden calf or money or power but with ourselves and what we can do, couched in ideologies both liberal and conservative. The actions to which students call their hearers are regularly well meaning and sometimes even noble. In fact, I think it is safe to say that I have never heard a student sermon that has called for doing harm, degrading anyone's humanity, or misusing creation. At the same time, when faith/trust in Jesus is relocated to trust in any other gods, even that which is noble becomes wicked, insofar as it invites the hearer—be they Christian already or someone just popping by to see what the Christians are up to today—to trust in something or someone other than Jesus Christ.

Faith, whatever its object, creates the world in which we live by conforming our imagination to its object. In terms of trusting in Jesus Christ, the imagination is formed to Christ. While it will take more digging later in the book (chapters 3 and 4), consider that such a formation of the imagination and reconciliation of the imagination to Christ is on par with Paul's teaching to the church in Corinth: "We have the mind of Christ" (1 Cor 2:16). Trusting in Jesus Christ conforms the imagination to Christ, faith's object, the fountain of living waters (Jer 2:13). In the words of the psalmist, "For with you is the fountain of life; in your light we see light" (Ps 36:9). In Christ's

8 Sincere apologies to my dear Roman readers for this intra-Protestant jab. All in good fun.

light, the imagination is illuminated, and through it, the world is reconciled in Christ Jesus.

Trusting anything else forms the imagination to something other than Christ. Trust in power for power's sake yields a world fixated on achieving and maintaining power while disregarding those without power or power's status. Trust in wealth for wealth's sake yields a world that worships accumulation and too easily identifies that which is and those that are disposable. Trust in death for death's sake yields a world that works very hard at avoiding the inevitable with a host of immortality projects that deny death and therefore disregard resurrection.[9] Trust in culture for culture's sake yields a world that values cultural conformity and shuns cultural diversity.[10] Trust in ideology for the ideology's sake yields a world that centers on a nouveau Gnosticism wherein people are defined by their ascent to a line of thinking.

These idols have captivated the imagination and competed for our trust for a long time. These shadow "churches" appear already in Scripture itself. From the beginning even. Consider that Adam and Eve come to cross-purposes with the Lord God because they, at the serpent's behest, want to be like God, able to differentiate *and therefore judge* between good and evil (Gen 3:5). The serpent, while wily, was truthful. What greater power is there than to be able to be like God? Worship of such a god by way of partaking of the sacrament of the fruit yields the dry rot by which all other dry rot is measured. There is a whole cast of biblical characters who play out this narrative of trusting that which is not God in search of power and security and rightness.

Consider the Israelites at the foot of Sinai, assembling their precious metals to forge a talisman for protection—the golden calf of golden calves. They felt powerless. Abandoned, even. Hippocrates, or someone smart like him, said that desperate times call for desperate measures.[11] So the Israelites, in their desperation and with religious

9 See Becker, *Denial of Death*.

10 Hear here a not-so-veiled reference to the biases that ideological criticisms (e.g., feminist, postcolonial) have exposed and helped correct.

11 See Hippocrates, *Aphorisms*, 1.6.

endorsement (cheers, Aaron!), form an inanimate object of gold in search of security, in search of power over uncertainty. Trusting in such a thing forms a world that might provide short-term comfort but does not yield life. Recall the psalmist again: "Those who make them are like them; so are all who trust in them" (Ps 115:3–8; see also Ps 135:15–18).

The church of wealth worships in the same sanctuary as the church of power. They might even have the same minister. This devotion is ancient and witnessed to in Scripture, from the never-fulfilled commandment of the Jubilee Year,[12] to warnings of the prophets,[13] to the still-contemporary issues about which the book of James teaches (Jas 2:2–7). While it is a theological error to say that God has a preference for the poor or the rich, it is absolutely accurate to say that wealth is not to be trusted and thereby worshipped because the by-product is violence to the poor.[14] When we worship at the churches of power and wealth, when we place our faith/trust in power and wealth as sources of health, healing, and wholeness, we—particularly our imaginations—are bound to be conformed to this. This church has an active and engaged membership, and we all might be on its rolls.[15]

---

12 Cf. Leviticus 25, which describes both the Sabbatical and the Jubilee Year. There is no evidence in any historical record that either was observed. Does this mean the Commandments are of no value? No. What it might well suggest is something about who God is and what God intends for what God has created, in spite of what we human beings intend for ourselves. Such a practice would bankrupt the churches of power and wealth and therefore upset the global economic applecart.

13 E.g., Amos 8:4–6.

14 God shows no partiality. Cf. Acts 10:34; Rom 2:11; Gal 2:6; and Eph 6:9.

15 Luther puts a point on this in his *Large Catechism*: "There are some who think that they have God and everything they need when they have money and property; they trust in them and boast in them so stubbornly and securely that they care for no one else. They, too, have a god—mammon by name, that is, money and property—on which they set their whole heart. This is the most common idol on earth. Those who have money and property feel secure, happy, and fearless, as if they were sitting in the midst of paradise. On the other hand, those who have nothing doubt and despair as if they knew of no god at all. We will find very few who are cheerful, who do not fret and complain, if they do

Perhaps the most insidious of the other gods, at least in the age of bad faith, is ideology. Ideology is the dry rot of most concern today. Ideology becomes a god when it displaces the gospel as the measure of truth and Jesus Christ, the gospel incarnate, as the ultimate object of our trust and therewith our imagination. In his commentary on Romans, Karl Barth put this quite clearly: "The gospel is not a truth among other truths. Rather, it sets a question-mark against all truths."[16] Any time the gospel is set as one truth among others, the church is rotting from the inside out. When ideologies, whether noble or wicked, displace the gospel of Jesus Christ, preaching becomes motivational speaking, the church worships itself, the study of Scripture becomes archeology, and theology is reduced to ethics.[17] Sometimes good comes of this. A church motivated by doing good is likely doing good. But this good can be is a new coat of paint obscuring dry rot. When ideology is misunderstood as good news, the church of Christ gives way to the church of the like-minded. The god of ideology is insidious.

This critique is an attempt neither to burn the church down nor to stand in the way of the good that the church does. By no means! At the same time, our imaginations and thus our actions are captive to gods.[18] This faith is bad faith. There is freedom in trusting in Jesus and the resulting reconciliation of the imagination to the crucified

---

not have mammon. This desire for wealth clings and sticks to our nature all the way to the grave"; *BC* 387.5–9.

16 Barth, *Epistle to the Romans*, 35.

17 Can a person be aware of their ideological ascent? There are different takes on this. Karl Marx, for example, would say that we can be aware. Following Jacques Lacan's line that the world is only known through the filter of language, Slavoj Žižek suggests that we cannot know the ideologies that we ascend to, not unlike a fish not knowing that they live in the water. Consider that it is both, especially when ideology gets instantiated in policy and, especially in the church, in ethics. See Žižek, *Sublime Object of Ideology*, 15–16.

18 Recall Jesus's words: "Then if any one says to you, 'Lo, here is the Christ!' or 'There he is!' do not *believe* it. For false Christs and false prophets will arise and show great signs and wonders, so as to lead astray, if possible, even the elect" (Matt 24:23–24 RSV).

and risen Christ. There is freedom in recentering our vision of the world from the place of trusting in Jesus Christ.

LET'S TALK IDEOLOGY

To better understand the age of bad faith, it is helpful to spill a bit of ink clarifying what is intended by the term *ideology*.

The delightfully wild and irreverent philosopher Slavoj Žižek (b. 1949) regularly tells a joke about the idolatry of ideology.[19] A patron at a restaurant orders a coffee without cream. Five minutes later, the waiter responds, "I'm sorry, sir. We are out of cream. Can I bring you a coffee without milk?" Ideology, no matter how absurd its cul-de-sac is, must be maintained. What is said is clearly absurd, and what is not said bespeaks the rigidity of the world envisioned by the ideology. No matter how obviously absurd the proposition is, one must maintain the facade that the proposition is viable, whether no cream or no milk. Given the current political atmosphere in which we are living, public discourse—whether between politicians or between patrons in pubs—often finds itself in such cul-de-sacs, with folks willing to shed blood, sometimes literally, over whether the coffee is without cream or without milk.

The term *ideology* spends most of its time with political philosophers but also hangs out with economic theorists, sociologists, and ethicists. While this term and its proponents, the *ideologues*, started with a neutral pursuit of the study of ideas at the dawn of the French Revolution (1789–99), it was not long before the term became derisive—something you hurl at those with whom you disagree. This derisiveness was initially directed at those expressing ideals that were critical of or alternative to the political status quo. The question that added coal to the fire was whether the political was pragmatic or theory driven. Did one put more stake in the situation

19 Žižek attributes the joke to the film *Ninotchka* (Ernst Lubitsch, 1939), a farce that plays upon the ideology of Leninist Russia in the early decades of the Soviet Union. The joke is told at minute 47.

of life in a village (e.g., little kids should have a place to play that keeps them from getting run over by the local stagecoach) or in a metatheory about how life should be in any village (e.g., little kids ought to have somewhere safe to play so that they don't get run over and thereby disrupt traffic flow)? To get a taste of the invective, reference was made in 1804 "to the fact that across the French debate the terms protestant, philosopher, encyclopedist, economist, principalist, idealogue, illuminist, jacobine, terrorist, and *homme de sang* were used synonymously."[20] Quite a motley crew! The negative connotations were perpetuated and heightened by Karl Marx (1818–83) and Friedrich Engels (1820–95) in the mid-nineteenth century, when they characterized ideology as "the instrument of the ruling classes, who asserted that their ideas were the ruling ideas and that [these ideas] legitimized the existing power relationships."[21] But Marx and Engels failed to see that their own program, which would become known as Marxism, was itself an ideology. To claim that a program of ideas was objective and scientific is shot through with holes—big holes. While it might well feel good for some to read this about Marx and Engels, the initiators of what would become the political theory and program of communism, recall the little parable about the speck and thc log.[22]

There was a movement after the end of World War II that claimed that the time of ideologies was coming to an end. This prediction coincided with what was seen as the demise of totalitarianism, a destructive ideology on steroids. Lots of steroids. Nazism would be the example par excellence. Hitler's death, however, did not kill his ideas, as we well know in the early twenty-first century, with Stalinism in tow and McCarthyism coming up the rear. Totalitarianism, as theory-become-policy, has popped up across the continents in our own day with clear "successes" in North Korea and Russia and a less successful but not less dangerous attempt in the United States that

20 Stråth, "Ideology and Conceptual History," 5.

21 Stråth, 8.

22 Cf. Matt 5:1–7; Luke 6:41–42.

I'll call Trumpism. Hegemonic ideologies are alive and not going away anytime soon.

A critical (both to the study of ideology and to the argument in this little book) recognition of ideology that has come in the last thirty years is that ideology is everywhere. All of us, you and I included, operate out of ideologies. It is not always conscious or written out, but it's there. Finnish historian Bo Stråth summarizes the transformation: "Ideologies are also everyday phenomena which we produce, disseminate, and consume throughout our lives. Ideologies make sense of the world and in this respect we cannot do without them, although they do not represent an objective external reality."[23]

Hence ideology is not only a pejorative term; it is a close cousin of worldview or metanarrative. What distinguishes an ideology is that it is a set of shared ideas that desire to make an impact on the present (e.g., group action and/or policy) with a particular vision of the future. The future that is envisioned is "better" than the present, at least for those who share the ideology.

Our current age is rife with ideologies from the nefarious to the well intentioned. The church—a human, this-worldly institution with a holy vocation—is not beyond the influence of ideology. Not now, not ever. To say that ideologies do not influence the church as an institution because it is the church amounts to self-deception. Abhorrent ideologies like white supremacy and other more clandestine forms of bigotry and prejudice such as tokenism distort the church's operation and proclamation. Similarly, the church's operation and proclamation are also impacted by more noble ideologies, such as radical inclusivity and environmentalism. There are many who will boo the former and cheer for the latter. If I had to choose, I would do the same. Except for one thing: the gospel of Jesus Christ. Now, given that I will have angered a good number of readers at this point, just hold on and keep reading. If you feel like I just called the church racist, you are correct, but keep reading. If you feel like I just

23 Stråth, "Ideology and Conceptual History," 17 (emphasis added). Stråth's reference is to Freeden, *Ideology*, 1.

put racism and radical inclusivity in the same kettle, you are correct, but keep reading.

Remember, ideologies *in the church* are most insidious gods.[24] They expect our trust and allegiance, and they expect imagination to conform to the object of the trust. Whether inside the church or out, anything that demands our trust either in place of or alongside Jesus Christ is a threat to trusting in Jesus, as it displaces Jesus Christ as Lord and Savior. In so doing, it yields bad faith—that is, trust in that which cannot provide what it claims: healing, wholeness, purity, peace, freedom. Such bad faith sets up a different measure of righteousness: trust in the ideology for health, healing, and wholeness. Such measures draw lines between who's in and who's out, between good and evil, between righteous and unrighteous. These lines based on intellectual ascent (i.e., agreement with the ideas and the future that they promise) threaten to reduce Christianity to a kind of Gnosticism.

Two caveats.

First, recall that Marx and Engels thought that their theories were beyond ideology. They critiqued ideologies with proper, observable truth. We have early twentieth-century sociologist Karl Mannheim (1893–1947) to thank for something that now bears his name: Mannheim's paradox, which states that one cannot expose a viewpoint as ideological without adopting an ideological viewpoint.[25] This observation is both helpful and challenging. It is helpful in that it acknowledges just how organic ideology is to how contemporary human beings make sense of the world and of time. Perhaps it would not be too much to say that there is no person who is beyond ideology. So with what ideology am I recognizing and critiquing the godlike nature of ideology in the church? Put another way, how can we tell the difference between bad faith and good?

It is important not to reduce trusting in Jesus Christ to an ideology while at the same time acknowledging that it bears a resemblance.

---

24 Consider Luke 16:15c.

25 Freeden, *Ideology*, 15.

This question will return down the road, but for the moment, consider bits of John's Gospel:

> You will know the truth, and the truth will make you free. (John 8:32)

> I am the way and the truth and the life. No one comes to the Father except through me. (John 14:6)

If Mannheim's paradox is accurate, then that which exposes ideology is the one who is the truth. This is, of course, a position of faith. It is an argument based on the triune God's self-revelation in Scripture rather than reason alone. Nevertheless, this is a book on theology, so this shouldn't be a huge surprise that Christology *rooted in trusting in Jesus Christ* is key.

Second, it is helpful to ponder briefly the gnosis movements in early Christianity. Gnosticism was not itself a full-blown, unified movement during the first centuries of the church. Rather it was something blowing in the wind throughout the Mediterranean and the Ancient Near East with examples in early Judaism and early Christianity as well as in the paganism of the day. In short, it was "a system which taught the cosmic redemption of the spirit through knowledge."[26] The parallels between contemporary worship of ideology and ancient Gnosticism should not be taken too far. For example, the common thread in the ancient Gnosticism of dualism—in reference to both cosmic powers and the human being's body (irredeemable) and spirit (redeemable)—is not the contemporary problem.[27] The problem *is* that redemption is dependent upon one's ascent to particular knowledge or ideas, which displace Jesus Christ, the incarnate, crucified, and risen Word made flesh, as Lord and Savior.

---

26 Pelikan, *Christian Tradition*, 1:82.

27 For a current snapshot of historical work on gnosis, cf. MacGuire, "Gnosis and Nag Hammadi," 204–26.

Recall again Barth's teaching: "The gospel is not a truth among other truths. Rather, it sets a question-mark against all truths."[28] We are all ideologues with sets of ideas and narratives and beliefs that we use—consciously and unconsciously—to make sense of the world. To write off this gospel question mark as either a liberal or a conservative agenda reduces the gospel to an ideology in concert with Mannheim's paradox. Rather, all Christians need to be mindful of the gospel question mark as we ponder the central calling of the Christian and of the church to trust in Jesus Christ.[29] Trusting in wealth or power or death or ideology is bad medicine (sorry for another Bon Jovi reference) and, as such, bad faith. This is the dry rot that endangers the church's witness to Jesus Christ.

Whether benevolent or hegemonic, those who steward the proclamation of the gospel, which is the lifeblood of the church, need to be wary of replacing the gospel of Jesus Christ with anything else.[30] Such a move, which happens regularly in pulpits of all denominations, at least in North America, is faithless. It reduces the church to a service organization and not the community of believers (i.e., trusters) in Jesus Christ. It turns the church into a community of the like-minded rather than those whose unity is in Jesus Christ alone. This is no bash on either service organizations or gatherings of the like-minded. Such groups are natural and part of the current state of human community. Such organizations often serve critical

---

28 Barth, *Epistle to the Romans*, 35.

29 Žižek does well opening up the Wizard of Oz–like nature of an ideology's object: "The sublime object is an object which cannot be approached too closely: if we get too near it, it loses its sublime features and becomes an ordinary vulgar object—it can persist only in an interspace, in an intermediate state, viewed from a certain perspective, half-seen. If we want to see it in the light of day, it changes into an everyday object, it dissipates itself, precisely because in itself it is nothing at all"; see Žižek, *Sublime Object of Ideology*, 192. The challenge for trusting in Jesus Christ is proclaiming and inhabiting Christ through faith in ways that mimic the ordinariness of the object of ideology unveiled.

30 "For we do not proclaim ourselves; we proclaim Jesus Christ as Lord" (2 Cor 4:5a).

functions in democratic societies.[31] The church, even in its fallen state, is not and cannot be such an organization. When it becomes such, it is a failure of the imagination of an organization (notice, *not church*) that has lost faith in Jesus Christ and is trusting in something else, usually itself and/or an ideology. The church becomes a house of bad faith. The primary girder that holds up the building is rotting from the inside out.

As for me and my house, I am far more familiar with the so-called mainline denominations. My own denomination, the Evangelical Lutheran Church in America, is no stranger to dry rot. We are the second whitest denomination in the United States. Officially formed on January 1, 1988, as a merger of three predecessor Lutheran bodies, this church in which I serve has been consciously trying to become more diverse for over thirty years. We have set goals and implemented policies to achieve greater diversity. And yet we have gone backward. In the process, we have (quite unintentionally, I like to think . . . but I'm also not immune from being wrong) institutionalized tokenism and continue to struggle with naming the fact that racism pervades our church from pews to pulpits to leadership to policy. Amid it all, we have poured theological resources into ethics, often relegating the activity of the triune God revealed in Jesus Christ and unveiled by the power of the Spirit to an assumption or afterthought.

Each denomination has its own story, its own theological matrix, its own accomplishment, its own sins. Denominations—no matter their claim—are but potsherds of the one, holy, catholic, and apostolic church, which is now and may always be invisible to the naked eye.[32]

In addition to the host of crises that the church is in, many of which the church has done to itself (e.g., child sex abuse and its cover-up, capitulation to hegemonic powers, quietism in the face of violence and injustice, irrationalism when faced with scientific discovery), this current dry rot is largely the result of a slippery slide

---

31 I assume that this is true in nondemocratic societies as well, but I have nothing upon which to base that assumption.

32 Cf. Nicene Creed, 381 CE, first article. See https://www.anglicancommunion.org/media/109020/Nicene-Creed.pdf.

into moralistic self-righteousness, whether the policy planks that preoccupy us be conservative or liberal.

I realize that this is starting to sound dire. I do not apologize for the tone or the content. Such admonishment is important to consider if it is the gospel of Jesus Christ that is primary. There are many other so-called gospels available for hire. This is nothing new. The "gospel according to humanity"[33] is not what the church is called to steward, and neither is "the human word."[34] We, the church, are stuck with the gospel according to Jesus Christ, whether we like it or not. We are called *in, by, and through trusting in Jesus Christ* to have the good of the neighbor *and of the enemy* in mind. The church, however, becomes just another service organization or club of the like-minded when trusting in Jesus as Lord and Savior as the center of life is lost.

Consider what Dietrich Bonhoeffer writes in *Life Together*, a book that is one part mystical vision and one part practical how-to of community in Christ Jesus: "We belong to one another only through and in Jesus Christ."[35] To get inside this interpretation of the centrality of trust in Jesus Christ on relationships and community, it is necessary to engage the imagination. Our attention turns to this later in the book—in the bits that hopefully contribute to the pursuit of an antidote to the dry rot, the topic of faith (trusting Jesus Christ) as mystical participation in the person and work of Jesus Christ, incarnate, crucified, and risen. Before turning in that direction, however, there are a few more aspects of the dry rot to consider—aspects that have more to do with life in these times, in particular the erosion of imagination and of public trust.

NO ESCAPING THE AIR WE BREATHE

Neither the church nor individual Christians live in a bubble. We live in the world and are of the world. We breathe the same air that

33 Cf. κατὰ ἄνθρωπον in 1 Cor 1:11.

34 Cf. λόγος ἀνθρώπων in 1 Thess 2:13.

35 Bonhoeffer, *Life Together*, 5:31.

our neighbor and our enemy breathe. We inhale the oxygen that plants and trees exhale. We drink the same water as the elephant, the cockroach, and the indigo bunting. We move and grow under the same conditions of gravity as the daffodil and the sequoia. Likewise, we are formed by other forces, other relationships, and other systems. All Christians, at least as far as I know, are earthlings.[36] So what is currently shaking on this little blue marble that is mixing with—perhaps even exacerbating—the bad faith? What other factors are at play with bad faith?

There are two phenomena that are part of the air we breathe right now (at least in North America, but the airflow seems to be global): a failure of trust, especially public trust, in the so-called posttruth era and with it the failure of imagination. The latter is explored in chapter 3. The former is largely beyond the scope of this study. Suffice it to say that there are strikingly creepy resonances between contemporary political rhetoric—at both national and grassroots levels—and an Orwellian world wherein language is eroded to prevent critical thought,[37] beauty is under attack,[38] and truth is

---

36 At the same time, it is fascinating to roll around in the question of life elsewhere in the cosmos in relation to the triune God.

37 The Party in Orwell's *1984* world was in the process of paring down language. "Oldspeak" was winnowed down to "Newspeak" to narrow the range of thought and illuminate "thoughtcrime." If people don't have the words to imagine the critique of the Party, which is thoughtcrime, then the Party and its ideology are beyond critique. For the conversation on "Newspeak" between Winston and Syme, cf. Orwell, *1984*, 49–58.

38 The Party's goal is absolute power directed toward a dystopia of pain and control—a vision where "there will be no laughter, except the laugh of triumph over a defeated enemy. There will be no art, no literature, no science. When we are omnipotent we shall have no more need of science. There will be no distinction between beauty and ugliness. There will be no curiosity, no enjoyment of the process of life. All competing pleasures will be destroyed. But always—do not forget this, Winston—always there will be the intoxication of power, constantly increasing and constantly growing subtler. Always, at every moment, there will be the thrill of victory, the sensation of trampling on an enemy who is helpless. If you want a picture of the future, imagine a boot stamping on a human face—forever." Orwell, 276–77.

but an instrument of those in power.[39] In the face of such attacks on truth, there is a critical axiom: "Freedom is the freedom to say that two plus two makes four. If that is granted, all else follows."[40] The freedom to call a thing what it is *is* essential to freedom itself. Posttruth and with it the failure of imagination are infections that weaken the body politic[41] and the body of Christ.[42]

With this in view, let me be perfectly clear: the Christian is not called to remove oneself from the world, to stop breathing the air. Asphyxiation is not the goal. These phenomena are part of living as a creature on planet Earth in the present. We're stuck with gravity as it is, and we need to breathe the air available. At the same time, we must consider what's in the air we're breathing.

---

39 Likewise, the Party controlled the order by squeezing the mind and imagination of autonomy: "If all others accepted the lie which the Party imposed—if all records told the same tale—then the lie passed into history and became truth. 'Who controls the past,' ran the Party slogan, 'controls the future: who controls the present controls the past'"; Orwell, 35–36.

40 In contrast to another slogan of the Party: "WAR IS PEACE FREEDOM IS SLAVERY IGNORANCE IS STRENGTH"; Orwell, 83.

41 McIntyre, *Post-truth*, is a helpful exploration of the phenomenon.

42 While addressing a different age with some striking similarities with the present, see Hancock, *Karl Barth's Emergency Homiletic.*

CHAPTER TWO

Faith as Trust

> Therefore, since we are justified by faith, we have peace with God through our Lord Jesus Christ.
>
> —Romans 5:1

> To be trusted is a greater compliment than being loved.
>
> —George MacDonald, *The Marquis of Lossie*

The word *faith* is generously sprinkled throughout the language of followers of Jesus as much today as it has been throughout the church's long and variegated history. Christians often say that faith is central to their lives as followers of Jesus. When asked what faith is, however, there is often a pause and a struggle to find the words.

Among churchy folk, the word tends to be an insider concept. This is both inevitable and unhelpful. All institutions, whether the post office, the local service club, any branch of the military, or the church, develop their own internal shorthand. Such shorthand, a hodgepodge of jargon and acronyms, helps the organization do what it does more efficiently, avoiding "laborious periphrasis."[1] Many

1 I take this little gem from the grammar I used learning ancient Greek when I was in college. The authors are making the argument for learning the insider grammatical jargon for words based on the kind and placement of accents in the words. For many years, it has stuck with me as a fine example of insider language: "A word bearing the acute upon the ultima is known as an oxytone, one with the acute upon the penult as a paroxytone, one with the acute upon the antepenult as a proparoxytone. One which bears the circumflex

institutions have onboarding programs for new folks with the goal of inviting people into their language and culture. In congregations, we call these programs Sunday school or Confirmation or new member classes. For public ministers of the gospel, we call it seminary. Repetitive participation in liturgy nurtures and sustains such language in the lives of many Christians. Like other institutions and organizations, we are not always very good at making this insider speak hospitable. Many congregations do things the way they have always been done and say things the way they have always been said, forgetting that the purpose of the church is to communicate the gospel clearly to the whole world, as if the windows and doors open for the world to hear and understand. We get used to "preaching to the choir," neglecting the reality that the key but abstract idea that the good news of Jesus is for all needs to be languaged in a way that all can actually hear.

Does this mean that we are not supposed to use the insider language of the church? Absolutely not. There is a richness in the church's language, whether the language of Scripture, the liturgy, prayers, or the hymns that we sing. Our responsibility, however, is to be mindful of this insider-outsider dynamic to the point that we *also* use language that translates key ideas into the vernacular of folks in the neighborhood, town, or city. Why? So that the gospel of Jesus might be heard and, through hearing, that folks might come to trust in Jesus and in so doing have life in Jesus's name.[2] Such evangelical hospitality also helps regular pew sitters, who benefit from the translation of Christianity's key concepts into a recognizable vernacular.

The focus of this chapter is to do just this with *faith in Jesus Christ.* The following exploration of faith in Jesus Christ pivots on the claim

---

upon the ultima is called a perispomenon, one with the circumflex upon the penult is a properispomenon. These terms, though formidable, will save much laborious periphrasis"; Chase and Phillips, *New Introduction to Greek*, 4. No doubt when such shorthand is shared among folks, it does avoid much laborious periphrasis. When it is not shared, however, it is a barrier to communication at the very least and probably inhospitable.

2 "*The Word* exists to be made known"; Wingren, *Living Word*, 13.

that faith can and should be languaged in ways that are not overtly churchy. To put it in a positive sense, this chapter attempts to cut to the heart of what faith is and argues that faith is accessible to all people.

FAITH IS TRUST

Translating faith as trust is a linguistically sound move. The Greek word πίστις, regularly translated as "faith" or "belief" in the New Testament, is at its core "trust."[3] Understanding faith as trust emphasizes that faith is a relationship. It is not a commodity. It is a relational dynamic.

It can be helpful to practice this when reading biblical texts. When reading Christian Scripture in English, simply replace the words *faith* and *belief* with *trust*, *believe* with *trust*, and *faithful* with *trustworthy*. Consider this well-known, beloved text as an illustration: "For God so loved the world that he gave his only Son, so that everyone who *believes* in him may not perish but may have eternal life" (John 3:16; emphasis added). In this much-beloved verse from John's Gospel, we have the word *believes*. This word in Greek is πιστεύων, a participle that is a cognate (i.e., a word that shares the same root as another) of the noun πίστις. So if faith is trust, consider that this verse also accurately reads, "For God so loved the world that he gave his only Son, so that everyone who [trusts] in him may not perish but may have eternal life." This subtle shift in language invites the reader/hearer into the idea that faith/belief is a relational reality. Shifting from *believes* to *trusts* does not domesticate the text, but it does put the text in a relational framework with which everyone is familiar.

---

3 For a thorough look at πίστις and the Latin *fides* in Scripture and the early church against the backdrop of the use of πίστις/*fides* in the world of the ancient Roman Empire, Teresa Morgan's study offers a breadth and depth of data and analysis; see Morgan, *Roman Faith and Christian Faith.*

Another text, this time from Paul's Epistle to the Romans: "For I am not ashamed of the gospel; it is God's saving power for everyone who believes, for the Jew first and also for the Greek. For in it the righteousness of God is revealed through *faith* for *faith*, as it is written, 'The one who is righteous will live by *faith*'" (Rom 1:16–17; emphases added).

These two verses—what can be considered the thesis of the whole of Romans—are chock full of faith language.[4] Similar to "believes" in John 3:16, these faith words are all cognates of πίστις. So if faith is trust, these verses also accurately read, "For I am not ashamed of the gospel; it is God's saving power for everyone who [trusts], for the Jew first and also for the Greek. For in it [that is, the gospel] the righteousness of God is revealed through [trust] for [trust], as it is written, 'The one who is righteous will live by [trust].'" To be clear, this text, like John 3:16, is theologically rich, like a theological chocolate tart with homemade whipped cream. It is the kind of text that one can ponder for a lifetime. Exchanging trust with faith does not empty the text of its depth or richness. Rather, the shift assists the reader/hearer in more fully savoring what Paul is talking about. Faith, central to the whole of Romans, is not a thing to be possessed. It is not a thing to be picked up and put down willy-nilly or a commodity that can be measured or bought and sold. Faith, which is trust, is *the key relationship* between the human being and the triune God.

HANGING OUT WITH HABAKKUK

Paul, as he is keen to do, draws what he is arguing about the gospel of Jesus Christ (of which he was not ashamed!) from what Christians traditionally call the Old Testament (OT).[5] This thesis statement for the Epistle to the Romans finds its way to its foundation, a quotation

4 E.g., Jewett, *Romans*, 135–36.

5 Christians share the Old Testament with our Jewish siblings, who refer to this collection of texts as Tanakh or Mikra. Often when Jews and Christians

from the prophet Habakkuk: "The one who is righteous shall live by [trust]" (Hab 2:4). Lest we think that πίστις is merely a New Testament concept, Paul grounds what he is proclaiming in what was Scripture for Jesus, Paul, and the rest of the early church—the Old Testament. Given that πίστις is a Greek word, what was Paul drawing on here? Well, Paul may have been translating from the Hebrew of Habakkuk, or he may have been working with a Greek translation of the Hebrew Bible (HB), commonly referred to as the Septuagint (LXX).[6]

For our purposes, it is important to be aware that the concept of faith as trust does not begin with the birth of Jesus. Paul, building the thesis of his Epistle to the Romans on a verse from Habakkuk, is emblematic of this. There is a continuity within Christian Scripture regarding the centrality of faith/trust as the relationship for which the triune God has created the human being (and, who knows, perhaps the worm, the whale, and the resident of another solar system as well).

In the LXX, πίστις and its cognates are the regular rendering of words that share the stem from the verbal root אמן (*aman*), which bespeaks a range of ideas: to believe, to trust, to persist, to establish.[7]

---

are studying these texts together and in scholarly work that includes both Jews and Christians, the collection is called the Hebrew Bible.

6 The most prominent Greek version of the OT/HB is regularly called the Septuagint, a reference to the second-century BCE story found in the Letter of Aristeas. This story, preserved in Greek, tells of seventy-two translators (six each from the twelve tribes of Israel) gathered in Alexandria who all translated the Torah from Hebrew into Greek sequestered from one another. When compared, their translations had no variations. This was portrayed as a miracle, a mark of the LXX's holiness and, therefore, authority. Now, the Letter of Aristeas is most likely a delightful legend, but the intention of the story is important here. The point of the story is that the Greek translation was inspired and therefore has a similar authority to the Hebrew. The LXX was the Scripture of the early church. There are a number of resources available to dig deeper into the early Greek translations of the Hebrew Bible—e.g., Dines, *Septuagint*; Jobes and Silva, *Invitation to the Septuagint*.

7 Another critical Hebrew word that renders as trust is בטח (*batach*), a trust that leans into reliance. The object of בטח can be God but is not necessarily so. By way of an example of the latter,

There are many cognates of the Hebrew root, more than we need to get into for the purpose of this little book. A few of the possibilities to put into your quiver for the next time you're playing Scrabble in Hebrew are אֱמוּנָה (*em-oo-NAH*, trust), אֹמֶן (*oh-MEN*, trustworthiness, faithfulness), אֱמֶת (*em-ETH*, truth, trust, trustworthiness), and אָמֵן (Amen!). The close relationship of *trust*, *trustworthiness*, *reliability*, and *truth* among the Hebrew cognates of אמן is worth keeping in mind.

Consider the verse from Habakkuk in context:

> Look at the proud!
> Their spirit is not right in them,
> but the righteous live by their [trust] [אֱמוּנָה, *emunah*].
> (Hab 2:4)

While the first half of this verse is a textual critic's sandbox and a head-scratcher for the rest of us, the second half of the verse is clear.[8] Within the large arc of Habakkuk, the first chapter is the prophet's lament at the situation of his people—besieged by the enemy from the outside and also besieged by an unrighteous wickedness on the inside. Hence the prophet cries to the Lord for help. The second chapter is the Lord's reply wherein the Lord basically lays out that there will be no tolerance of wickedness, injustice, and idolatry. This little bit (Hab 2:4b) sets out the Lord's singular promise: the righteous

> O Lord of hosts,
> happy is everyone who trusts in you. (Ps 84:12)

And of the former,

> They shall be turned back and utterly put to shame—
> those who trust in carved images,
> who say to cast images,
> "You are our gods." (Isa 42:17)

8 As with many verses, there are a few ways the text can be read given that there are a variety of extant textual witnesses and text traditions. Hab 2:4a is particularly challenging to sort out, as none of the variants are clearly *the right one*.

shall live by their faith/trust. Idolatry, whether of power or wealth or good old-fashioned idols made of clay, marks the unrighteous. Trust in the Lord, however, marks the righteous and is the animation of being. That is, trust in the Lord is life.

It is interesting to also consider how the LXX renders Habakkuk 2:4b: ὁ δὲ δίκαιος ἐκ πίστεώς μου ζήσεται.[9] In English, this roughly translates as "But the righteous one will live by my faith/faithfulness." While the LXX translates אֱמוּנָה with a form of πίστις, there is an interesting difference in the Greek: the pronoun *my*. In the context of Habakkuk, the speaker is clearly the Lord. So while the Hebrew declares that the righteous one will live by their own faith/trust, the Greek declares that the righteous one will live by the faithfulness/trustworthiness of the Lord.[10] Lucky for us, both are theologically true when the dynamics of the relationship of trust are considered. Trust and trustworthiness go hand in glove in any relationship. As noted earlier, we humans are the trusters, and the triune God is the Trustworthy One. While I do not want to downplay this textual difference too much, it remains interesting and worth further exploration. For our purposes, both options have resonance with the centrality of faith/trust in the Christian life, which follows from the trustworthiness of the triune God. Then again, when Paul quotes Habakkuk 2:4b, he omits any pronoun at all.

While faith/trust is not the only motif of Habakkuk, faith does make another appearance that is illustrative of Habakkuk's emphasis on faith. In Habakkuk 1, which is the prophet's lament about how wickedness prevails in Judah, awakening the ire of the Lord, the prophet says, "For a work is being done in your days that you would not believe if you were told" (Hab 1:5b). The work to which Habakkuk refers is that the Lord is raising up the Chaldeans to exercise divine judgment upon the Judeans. This work of the Lord is so wild

9 Throughout this volume, LXX texts are taken from the critical edition compiled by Alfred Rahlfs, *Septuaginta*.

10 For a brief résumé of the centrality of Hab 2:4b in both Jewish and Christian interpretation, cf. Coggins and Han, *Six Minor Prophets*, 61–65, with an excursus on Augustine's interpretations of Hab 2:4b (see 71–73).

that it's unimaginable! Would the Lord do such a thing? There is a confluence of the two primary foci of this book here: imagination and faith. The Lord's sovereignty is such that the Lord is free to do that which is unbelievable because it is unimaginable. This wildly free sovereignty is also the place from which the Lord says in 2:4b that the righteous one will live by trust.

Beyond Habakkuk, trust (humans) and trustworthiness (God) are threads woven throughout the Old Testament tapestry. Indeed, faith/trust in God alone who is trustworthy is the theological telos of the Old Testament witness.[11]

Returning to the appearance of this verse in Paul's Epistle to the Romans, "For I am not ashamed of the gospel; it is God's saving power for everyone who believes, for the Jew first and also for the Greek. For in it the righteousness of God is revealed through faith for faith, as it is written, 'The one who is righteous will live by faith'" (Rom 1:16–17).[12] While in contemporary biblical scholarship, Paul's quoting of Habakkuk out of context is at times frowned upon as a disservice to the OT text, such judgment is anachronistic. Linguistic resonance (shared language) was of primary consideration with historical/narrative context of lesser interpretive value.[13] Paul's goal in Romans is to sort out how both Jews and Gentiles relate to the God of Israel in light of God's self-revelation in the incarnation, death, and resurrection of Jesus Christ. Drawing from Daniel Harrington, "As a first-century Jew, Paul certainly regarded what we call the Old Testament as possessing great authority. Nevertheless, Paul's primary authority was his own encounter with the risen Christ whom he believed he had experienced on the road to Damascus."[14]

In a preview of what will come (chapter 5), we see in Romans 1 the germination of the imagination of faith, which is arrived at not through willy-nilly, fanciful eisegesis but through the text "in and through faith in Jesus Christ." Trust grounded in the Christ event

11 Cf. Giere, "Faith and the Lord's Making-New," 25–30.

12 In addition to Rom 1:17, see also Gal 3:11 and Heb 10:38.

13 Cf. Giere, *New Glimpse of Day One.*

14 Harrington, "Paul's Use," CP1.

is the normative lens through which Paul's interpretive imagination of faith reads Scripture and articulates the promise. Indeed, Paul's interpretation and use of Habakkuk 2:4b is the imagination of faith *in Jesus Christ* at work.

TRUST AND TRUSTWORTHINESS

Understanding faith as trust opens the horizon of this central theological concept in ways that can help flesh out the place of faith in the Christian life and also who God reveals God's self to be in Christian Scripture—the Trustworthy One.

Trust is a fundamental dynamic of every human relationship extending back to times before recorded history and before memory.[15] Whether thinking about the instinctual bond between mother and infant or about the elements necessary to begin to build communities of interdependent people, trust plays a key role in the most basic aspects of life together as human beings.

Life together here is key, as trust is relational.[16] There are at least two actors involved: person X trusts person Y. In this relationship, X trusts *because* Y is trustworthy. There is a third factor in this relationship that is also important. It is the "for what task" of the trusting. That is, X trusts Y for Z. (Hold on just a bit longer with this, especially for those who have broken out in a cold sweat given the similarity to algebra.) Z might be everything, or Z might be something limited and specific. For example, imagine a relationship between an infant and her mother, which we will assume for the moment is a healthy and wholesome relationship. X is the infant, and

15 While this might seem an outrageous claim that lacks evidence from a time when there is no evidence, the essential nature of trust and the value of trustworthiness to human community and thriving throughout recorded history suggest that the dynamic of trust germinated in the history of human beings prior to that history being recorded.

16 Consider the following resources for exploring the philosophy of trust more thoroughly: Hawley, *How to Be Trustworthy*; Hawley, *Trust*; Hardin, *Trust and Trustworthiness*; and Simon, *Routledge Handbook*.

Y is the mother.[17] When this relationship is a healthy and wholesome relationship, Y is trustworthy in every way. When the baby poops herself, the mother changes the diaper. When the baby is hungry, the mother feeds her. When the baby feels alone, the mother cuddles her. When the baby is scared, the mother comforts her. In this example, Z would be everything. In fact, the infant, who has very little agency in terms of caring for herself, has no choice but to trust her mother for everything.

More often, when X trusts Y for Z, the "for what" is more specific.

Consider another example. Imagine that X is me, the author of this little book; Y is my gastroenterologist; and Z is a colonoscopy. (I recently turned fifty. It's on my mind. Sorry.) In this case, Z is quite specific in terms of what I am trusting my doctor to do and do well. Given that my gastroenterologist is board certified and in good standing with the folks who say that a doctor is good enough to practice medicine, they have vouched for the doc's trustworthiness. It is reasonable for me to trust the doctor *for a colonoscopy*. It is unreasonable for me to trust in the doctor for a home improvement project or for friendship or for a haircut or even for removing a brain tumor. Might my gastroenterologist be trustworthy for any of these other things? Perhaps. Shoot, my gastroenterologist might be my best friend. In the proposed scenario, however, Z is a colonoscopy that is safe, successful, and informative. Likewise, it would be unreasonable for me to entrust myself to my barber for this same colonoscopy.

All this is to say that trust is relational: X → Y. The trust of X depends on the trustworthiness of Y. And it is quite reasonable that trust and trustworthiness are limited to a particular "for what" Z.

To complicate matters, there are several other dynamics to this X → Y for Z relationship. Consider the following:

- What if X's trust in Y for Z is unreasonable?
- What if X does not clearly communicate Z to Y?

---

17 To be clear, this is a positive example of trust that is in no way intended to be exclusive of the father's role.

- What if Y promises X to do Z but does not follow through with Z (or any other letter of the alphabet!)?

To say that faith is trust does not make faith simplistic. Rather, to say that faith is trust places faith in a complex orbit that we all as human beings in relationship with other human beings negotiate every day of our lives. Consider some examples of the complexity.

What if X's trust in Y for Z is unreasonable? You end up going to your barber for your colonoscopy. This is dangerous and daft. While the barber might have a gold medal from the Olympics of barbering, and he may have even had a colonoscopy himself, he is not competent to perform the procedure and should not be trusted to do so. It would be unreasonable to seek such a procedure from my barber, and in the likely event that the barber made a mess of the colonoscopy, it would be equally unreasonable for me to feel betrayed by the failure.

What if X does not clearly communicate Z to Y? If I expect my spouse to pay the electrical bill but I communicate it vaguely or not at all, miscommunication would result not only in an overdue bill but also perhaps in damage to the relationship. In this case, I have eroded my partner's ability to trust me because of my poor communication of Z.

What if Y promises to do Z but does not follow through? If I ask a friend to look after my dog while I'm away for a couple of days and the friend says "Sure thing!" but fails to follow through with the commitment, what results? Not only do I end up cleaning up piles of dog shit around my house, but my ability to trust the friend is damaged. The friend has proved untrustworthy, at least in terms of following through with a stated commitment (Z). They are unreliable. The relationship is damaged. And lest we forget the puppy, the dog is at least hungry, and the poor thing's trust in me, its owner, might well be damaged by this neglect.

While there are good reasons *not* to trust someone, sometimes there are good reasons to trust someone for something specific. I (X) might trust someone (Y) who is sketchy and untrustworthy because we have a mutual interest that raises the likelihood that they will follow through with Z. If a friend is completely worthy of trust in matters of life and death, I (X) am right to entrust my life (Z) to them (Y) in such situations. If the same friend (Y) is an absolute butterfingers—let's say a person who I have witnessed drop and break a host of things—it would be foolish of me (X) to entrust this same person (Y) with my Royal Doulton china (Z).[18]

Given the complexities related to the equation X → Y for Z, you might be thinking that this shift from faith to trust is not worth it. Let's continue with *faith* and leave well enough alone. Fair enough, but hold on just a bit. There is a difference between something being simplified and something being simplistic. Faith as trust is not simplistic. In fact, considering faith as trust opens some aspects of faith that we might not otherwise consider. As mentioned earlier, *trust* is a word that refers to a relational dynamic that each of us experiences all the time. Trust is relational.[19] Not in an idealistic sense but in a realistic sense. This means that the idea of trust necessarily includes the idea of trustworthiness, with the value of trustworthiness being paramount.[20] Trust must also consider mistrust and untrustworthiness. Trust must consider the difference between trust and mere reliance.[21] Trust must consider concepts like promise, reliability, competence, relational longevity, gullibility, implicit bias, danger, courage, safety, community, and so on.

Returning to an earlier example, trust like that between a mother and child is a beautiful thing. At the same time, even this most intimate trust can be betrayed. We humans have a great capacity

18 Yes. This is a not-so-subtle nod to the interactions between Hyacinth Bucket (pronounced BOO-que—played by Patricia Routledge) and her neighbor Elizabeth (Josephine Tewson) on the BBC sitcom *Keeping Up Appearances* in the early 1990s.

19 "How we understand each of trust and trustworthiness shifts in synch with how we understand the other"; Scheman, "Trust and Trustworthiness," 28.

20 Hawley, *How to Be Trustworthy*, 72.

21 Trust is a thicker relationship, whereas reliance is more transactional. Katherine Hawley helps distinguish the two by reactions to broken trust and broken reliance: "Our reaction to misplaced trust (betrayal) differs from our reaction to misplaced reliance (disappointment)"; Hawley, *How to Be Trustworthy*, 4.

for ruining something wholesome and life-giving. The mind does not need to wander far for examples, whether they be interpersonal or corporate.

But if the conversation about faith as trust is restricted to the realm of anthropology—that is, trust as a relational dynamic between people—then there are a thousand cul-de-sacs in which to get stuck. To say that faith is trust does not remove the human element from that which is holy (Col 1:21–23; Jude 20–21) and wholly given by God: "For by grace you have been saved through [trust, πίστις], and this is not your own doing; it is the gift of God—not the result of works, so that no one may boast" (Eph 2:8–9). Given the dynamics of trust and trustworthiness, consider that the giftedness of faith/trust is the trustworthiness of the triune God. In the church, we call this trustworthiness by several names; primarily, it is the good news of Jesus Christ or the gospel. We envision it as deliverance from slavery; as suffering servant; as eternal, incarnate Word; as crucified and risen Christ; as tongues of fire; as the risen Jesus serving up some broiled fish for breakfast on the beach. We intone this in our liturgies and hymns. We receive this trustworthiness with hands open and outstretched as beggars at the Lord's table with the words *for you.*

THE TRUSTWORTHINESS OF THE TRIUNE GOD

Like trust relationships, our trust in the triune God can be fickle. Given the fine line between sin and faith (see chapter 1), we human beings are quite keen to entrust ourselves to that which is not God, to trust in idols of our making. Recall Psalm 115:

> Our God is in the heavens;
>   he does whatever he pleases.
> Their idols are silver and gold,
>   the work of human hands.
> They have mouths, but they do not speak;
>   they have eyes, but they do not see.

They have ears, but they do not hear;
  they have noses, but they do not smell.
They have hands, but they do not feel;
  they have feet, but they do not walk;
  they make no sound in their throats.
Those who make them are like them;
  so are all who trust in them. (Ps 115:3–8)[22]

The psalmist is talking about *their* idols—that is, those of the nations (Ps 115:2). Some good ol' fashioned finger wagging. Against the backdrop of Scripture as a whole, however, it is clear that the psalmist and everyone—you and me included!—have their own idols. Recall Calvin: the human being's "nature . . . is a perpetual factory of idols."[23] These idols, of course, are not limited to ones made of precious metals or even by human hands. The key here is that our idols are not ultimately trustworthy. While they might be gratifying in the short term, they cannot deliver the promises we project upon them. By way of example, an idol that gets worshipped regularly in large swaths of American Christianity, the family, is not essentially an idol, but it can be idolized.[24] When we idolize something—that is, when we place our trust in that something for life and wholeness—it becomes dead and takes us with it. *Those who make them are like them; so are all who trust in them.*

We humans are inclined to forge idols for ourselves. Key to moving the conversation forward is shifting focus from *our trust* to God's

22 Also 135:15–18.

23 *Institutes* I.11.8. Calvin is alluding to Pss 115 and 135. The context of this comment is Calvin's discussion of images of God, which touches on what Calvin describes as the wickedness of the imagination: "Man's mind, full as it is of pride and boldness, dares to imagine a god according to its own capacity; as it sluggishly plods, indeed is overwhelmed with the crassest ignorance, it conceives an unreality and an empty appearance as God. To these evils a new wickedness joins itself, that man tries to express in his work the sort of God he has inwardly conceived. Therefore the mind begets an idol; the hand gives it birth" (I.11.8).

24 Yes, this is a cheap shot at Dobson's organization, Focus on the Family, which regularly elevates a narrow cultural ideal of "family" to an idol.

trustworthiness. After all, our trust in God is a by-product of God's trustworthiness. Ultimately, this whole kit and caboodle is about who God is and what God has done. The psalmist speaks of this:

> Not to us, O Lord, not to us, but to your name give glory,
> for the sake of your steadfast love and your faithfulness.
> (Ps 115:1)

Hence the story to be told is not first about our fickle trust. It is the story of the Lord's trustworthiness—that is, the *Lord's* steadfast love and faithfulness. Who the triune God reveals God's self to be is the keystone that makes the rest true and functional.[25] The Lord's trustworthiness is rooted in the primary creation story for Christians, the prologue to John's Gospel: "In the beginning was the Word, and the Word was with God, and the Word was God. He was in the beginning with God; all things were made through him, and without him was not anything made that was made. In him was life, and the life was the light of [people]. The light shines in the darkness, and the darkness has not overcome it. . . . And the Word became flesh and dwelt among us, full of grace and truth; we have beheld his glory, glory as of the only Son from the Father" (John 1:1–5, 14 RSV). In what might be passed over as a flowery preamble, we have the cornerstone of God's self-revelation. The incarnation of the Word, which reaches its telos or completion in Christ's crucifixion and death,[26] is the point at which God reveals most clearly God's commitment to the cosmos.[27] Indeed, in and through Christ Jesus, God has reconciled the cosmos to God (2 Cor 5:19). That is, the incarnation, death, and resurrection of Jesus Christ, the eternal, incarnate Word, are the triune God's trustworthiness.[28] While our trust in God's trustwor-

25 Giere, "Eighth-Day Kiss," 10–13.

26 The incarnation of the eternal Word incarnate "is perfected on the cross"; Aulen, *Faith of the Christian Church*, 210.

27 In concert with the whole of Christian Scripture.

28 Consider Ian A. McFarland's "unreserved Chalcedonianism": "In response to various alternatives that have been proposed in the modern period, I have defended a 'Chalcedonianism without reserve,' by which I mean an

thiness remains fickle, God's trustworthiness remains constant, dependable.

As discussed earlier, when considering trustworthiness, it is quite right to remember X → Y for Z. The Lord's trustworthiness depends on the Lord fulfilling Z. So what is Z? For this, we need to turn back to the idea of faith within Christianity.

USES OF *FAITH* WITHIN THE CHURCH

Faith is trust. Faith is also faith. That is, faith cannot be extracted from the church's discourse, history, and present. Faith is everywhere from the ancient liturgies of the church to the cheeseball songs in Vacation Bible School curricula. So what does the church mean by faith? There are at least three ways the church uses *faith*.

The first use of faith is what this little book is pursuing: trusting in Jesus Christ. This is the faith that by God's grace makes the sinner righteous. Recall Ephesians 2:8: "For by grace you have been saved through faith [trust], and this is not your own doing; it is the gift of God." This is the faith that frees the person from the ultimately empty pursuit of life, healing, and wholeness by means of trusting that which cannot provide life. This faith, in the spirit of trusting, is relational, grounded upon the trustworthiness of God. This faith is participation in the incarnation, death, and resurrection of Jesus Christ.

---

insistence that because Jesus of Nazareth is the Word made flesh, God is fully present and truly known in Jesus' humanity. This is good news because although we are always present to God by virtue of God's role as Creator, who sustains us in our being at every moment of our being, only by taking flesh does God become present to us by coming to be with us, making it possible for human life to be lived with (rather than merely under) God. Moreover, since the communion thereby achieved overcomes all that would separate us from God (Rom. 8:31–39), these considerations lead me to conclude that one virtue of an unreserved Chalcedonianism is its ability to give full expression to the biblical conviction that 'in Christ God was reconciling the world to himself' (2 Cor. 5:19)"; McFarland, *Word Made Flesh*, 213–14.

The second use of faith is the statement of who this triune God reveals God's self to be for the world. Throughout the life of the church, this has been known by the shorthand expression "the rule of faith" (*regula fidei*). *Rule* here means a ruler or a measure. What is being measured? The basic content of who God is: one God who is Father, Son, and Holy Spirit. One God, three persons. From the early days of the church, the rule of faith has been associated with baptism, the sacrament by which the person through water and promise enters into Christ's death and life (Rom 6:3–5). Prior to baptism, the person professes their faith (trust) in the triune God with an accepted summary of the heart of who God has revealed God's self to be, a summary of the triune God's being and trustworthiness. Christians have called these *creeds*, from the Latin verb *credere*, to trust or believe. The candidate for baptism was asked three questions: Do you believe in God the Father? Do you believe in Jesus Christ, the Son of God? Do you believe in God the Holy Spirit? To each question, the response was and remains, *I believe . . . Credo . . . Πιστεύω . . . I trust. . . .* The Apostles' Creed, spoken in the first-person singular, is the baptismal creed, which provides the content of the profession of faith into whose name the person is being baptized. In a world where *god* is vague and has a multiplicity of meanings, the profession of faith/trust in the triune God indicates that this event is particularly Christian. The Nicene Creed of 381 CE, spoken in the first-person plural—*We believe . . . Credimus . . . Πιστεύομεν. . . .*—is the church's corporate confession of faith/trust in the triune God. It is known as the ecumenical creed, as it is shared most broadly among Christians around the world. The creeds, as articulations of the rule of faith, while not in Scripture, are of Scripture. Martin Luther captured this poetically when writing about the place of the creed in relation to Scripture and within the life of the Christian: "This confession of faith we did not make or invent, neither did the fathers of the church before us. But as the bee gathers the honey from many a beautiful and delicious flower, so this creed has been collected in commendable brevity from the books of the beloved prophets and apostles, that is, from the entire Holy Scriptures, for children and plain Christians."[29]

Christian Scripture exists in a symbiotic relationship with the rule of faith. At certain intersections, there is harmony; at others, there is discord. Either way, the symbiosis is persistent and true. Theology emerges as the church reflects upon and speaks about this symbiosis, the measure of who God has revealed God's self to be. Anselm of Canterbury (1033–1109 CE) described this movement as "faith seeking understanding" (*fides quaerens intellectum*). The rule of faith remains the basis of this second use of "faith" as the person or community explores the implications and impacts of God's self-revelation for the world.

A third use of the word *faith* is as a synonym for Christianity as a whole—for example, "the Christian faith."[30] Perhaps the only relevance of this definition of this exploration is the inherent nod to the centrality of "faith" that such shorthand suggests. This whole Christian enterprise, from the standpoint of the human being, is faith. Granted, this is a flimsy observation, as "faith" is interpreted in several different ways and given a variety of different priorities within the grab bag of theological systems within the church ecumenical. So be it.

The two definitions of concern are the first and second. The first is relational faith, which is trust. Since trust that justifies is relational, the second definition of faith—that is, the rule of faith—is also critical, as it is the expression of God's trustworthiness.

---

29 Plass, *What Luther Says*, 1.352; see also WA 41.275.

30 This use of faith is often applied inappropriately by Christians to other religions. It is an incorrect superimposition to refer to the Buddhist "faith," as faith is a Christian concept. It is better that we refer to world religions rather than world faiths.

JESUS TRANSFORMS WHAT FOLKS BRING INTO FAITH

Much of our understanding of faith as trust comes from the writings of the apostle Paul, as faith is the central, driving concept of his writings.[31] But what does Jesus have to say about faith?

In the Synoptic Gospels,[32] Jesus regularly says something to the effect of "Your faith has made you well."[33] A common thread that runs through these encounters is that folks in desperate situations seek healing, restoration from Jesus. Why from Jesus? That's up for debate. The story of the so-called hemorrhaging woman is a brief tale, embedded with different layers like a Russian doll (*matryoshka*), of the resuscitation of the daughter of an important person.[34] In each of the tellings, the hemorrhaging woman is described as a social outcast who is desperate and unable to be healed physically.[35] All three versions convey that she suffered from the hemorrhage for twelve years, with Matthew and Luke providing the insight that she had sought healing but was unable to be cured by anyone (Luke 8:43). Matthew and Mark actually give us insight into the woman's motivation as the reader is invited to hear her thoughts: "If I but touch his cloak, I will be made well" (Mark 5:28).[36] Her thoughts confirm her desperation.

What is it that she believes about who this Jesus is? She makes no confession of him as Messiah or as Son of God. In her desperation, she searches for healing and restoration. She seeks the help of others—physicians, according to Mark's version. Having exhausted other means, she seeks to touch this holy man's garment. His power

---

31 "Faith is the central concept used to denote the human correlate of the eschatological redemptive reality revealed in Christ"; Ridderbos, *Paul*, 738.

32 Matthew, Mark, and Luke are often called the *Synoptic Gospels* because of their striking similarity, *synoptic* meaning roughly "seeing together."

33 E.g., Matt 8:13; 9:22; 9:29; 15:28; Mark 5:34; 10:52; Luke 7:50; 8:48; 17:19; 18:42.

34 Cf. Matt 9:18–26; Mark 5:21–43; Luke 8:40–56.

35 All three Gospels reference a "ruler" (ἄρχων). Mark and Luke clarify that the ruler was of the synagogue, with Luke adding that his name was Jairus.

36 Also Matt 9:21.

to heal was likely the chatter about town, but it does not matter to her whence the power came; she needs it. And so, as if reaching out for the magical, from the midst of the crowd, she touches the hem of Jesus's garment. When she touches Jesus's garment, the hemorrhage ceases immediately. She is healed. While the tellings recall Jesus's reaction a bit differently, Jesus's verbal response to the woman is nearly the same in each: "Daughter, your faith has made you well; go in peace, and be healed of your disease" (Mark 5:34).[37]

Jesus declares that her desperation is faith. Jesus transformed whatever it was that brought her to this point of seeking the hem of his garment into trust—that is, saving, healing, life-giving faith. When someone is occupying the fragile place between life and death, Jesus transforms desperation, magical thinking, even grief into faith by merely saying that it is so.[38]

YE OF LITTLE FAITH

All this said about those who seek Jesus out of desperation, what of those closest to Jesus? The disciples? We religious leaders today?

While Jesus's generosity toward the desperate seems without measure, his patience with those closest to him can be pretty thin. Consider the scene that shows up in all three Synoptics where Jesus and his disciples are on a boat ride to the other side of the lake.[39] Jesus falls asleep. A storm brews. The disciples, some of whom are seasoned sailors, are terrified. They wake Jesus to let him know that they are perishing. Their desperation is clear in each version:

---

37 Also "Take heart, daughter; your faith has made you well" (Matt 9:22), and "Daughter, your faith has made you well; go in peace" (Luke 8:48).

38 Recall C. S. Lewis's words: "You never know how much you believe anything until its truth or falsehood becomes a matter of life and death to you. It is easy to say you believe a rope to be strong and sound as long as you are merely using it to cord a box. But suppose you had to hang by that rope over a precipice. Wouldn't you then first discover how much you really trusted it?" Lewis, *Grief Observed*, 10.

39 Cf. Matt 8:23–27; Mark 4:35–41; Luke 8:22–25.

> Lord, save us! We are perishing! (Matt 8:25)
>
> Teacher, do you not care that we are perishing? (Mark 4:38)
>
> Master, Master, we are perishing! (Luke 8:24)

There is existential terror evident in all three. All three versions have the disciples using the same verb for their plight. They say, *We are being utterly destroyed* (ἀπολλύμεθα)! There's really no less desperation in the words of the disciples in this story than in the woman with the hemorrhage. Yet to her, Jesus declares that whatever motivation it was that caused her to simply want to touch his clothes was her faith, her trust that Jesus had some kind of power to heal. To the disciples, those closest to him, he responds with,

> Why are you afraid, you of little [trust]? (Matt 8:26)
>
> Why are you afraid? Have you still no [trust]? (Mark 4:40)
>
> Where is your [trust]? (Luke 8:25)

This vignette of an evening boat ride functions like the Gospels, as whole narratives, function. It communicates who Jesus is. The primary point of this story is that Jesus has the power to calm the wind and the sea. Each of the three versions ends with the disciples in a state of awe asking a variation of the question, *Who is this that even the wind and sea obey him?*[40] But what about Jesus's different response to the disciples than to the woman who was hemorrhaging? Given the number of times that Jesus says something like "Where is your trust?" (Luke 8:25)[41] to his inner circle, there is something here worth noting. Consider that for those on the inside, for those who hear about and taste and see the trustworthiness of Jesus Christ, there

40 Matt 8:27; Mark 4:41; Luke 8:25.

41 Also "folks of little faith" (ὀλιγόπιστος); cf. Matt 6:30; 8:26; 14:31; 16:8; Luke 12:28.

is an expectation of trust. Or perhaps it is some divine befuddlement at the consistent lack of trust by those closest to Jesus, those among whom the full trustworthiness of God is present and active.[42]

TRUSTING IN JESUS IS THE POINT

In John's Gospel, trust in Jesus Christ is the whole point of the story.

In theater and film, there is the storytelling convention called "breaking the fourth wall," whereby a character in the story speaks directly to the audience, subverting the invisible barrier between the tale and listeners. Often this storytelling move is intended to give the character's first-person insight into a portion or aspect of the story or into the scene's place in the narrative arc of the whole. A payoff of the technique is that it invites the audience into active and involved participation in the story.

Something like a fourth-wall break happens at the end of John's Gospel. In the wake of the empty tomb and resurrection appearances (John 20) that function to seal the glorification that happened when Jesus was lifted up onto the cross and crucified, John, the storyteller, turns to the audience and sums up the story: "Now Jesus did many other signs in the presence of the disciples, which are not written in this book; but these are written that you may believe that Jesus is the Christ, the Son of God, and that believing you may have life in his name" (John 20:30–31 RSV).

John's rich telling of Jesus's story, which begins before time, finds its purpose statement with this fourth-wall break very near the end of the book. John, for this moment, is not narrating Jesus's story as much as he's inviting the audience into the intended impact of the story, this grand tale of creation and redemption. John reveals the why: "These are written that you may believe that Jesus is the

42 Consider Jesus's frustration with the disciples in the story of the healing of the boy with epilepsy; cf. Matt 17:14–20; Mark 9:14–29; Luke 9:27–43a.

Christ, the Son of God, and that believing you may have life in his name" (John 20:31 RSV).[43]

Operating with the idea that faith is trust, consider reading it a bit differently: *These are written that you may **trust** that Jesus is the Christ, the Son of God, and that **trusting** you may have life in his name.* The intention of John's Gospel is to trust in Jesus Christ, "that Jesus is the Christ, the Son of God."[44] And trusting in Jesus Christ yields life in Jesus's name. Trusting in Jesus and life go hand in glove. This telling of the gospel, the good news of Jesus Christ, the narration of the trustworthiness of the triune God revealed in Jesus Christ, *yields trust, and trust yields life.*

In fact, in John's Gospel, faith/trust is clearly about the relationship between the human being and the triune God. Statistics never tell the whole story, but they can help discern the texture of something. In the Gospel of John, *faith/trust* as a verb appears ninety-eight times. Whereas the noun πίστις does not make a single appearance.[45] The texture of faith/trust is one of relational motion,[46] a reality that is alive. As the end of John 20 says, a living trust that Jesus, the Christ,[47] is the Son of God not only *is the point* of the storytelling of the triune God's trustworthiness but *is the Christian life.* In fact, trusting in Jesus *is life in his name.*

---

43 In Greek: ταῦτα δὲ γέγραπται ἵνα πιστεύητε ὅτι Ἰησοῦς ἐστιν ὁ χριστὸς ὁ υἱὸς τοῦ θεοῦ, καὶ ἵνα πιστεύοντες ζωὴν ἔχητε ἐν τῷ ὀνόματι αὐτοῦ.

44 Given textual variants, it is possible that this is either or both of the following: an evangelical promise (that you might come to trust) or an encouragement to preserve in trust (that you might continue to trust). Cf. Hurtado, *God in New Testament*, 109.

45 The adjectival form, πιστός, does appear once in the Thomas story (John 20:24–29) in contrast with lacking trust: "Put your finger here, and see my hands; and put out your hand, and place it in my side; do not be distrustful (perhaps do not be leery), but be trusting" (v. 29).

46 "When faith is *faith in Christ* it contains . . . a constant motion, the motion away from ourselves to Christ"; Prenter, *Spiritus Creator*, 108.

47 To say that Jesus is "the Christ" is to say that Jesus is the Messiah, the Anointed One of the God of Israel.

TRUSTING IN JESUS IS PARTICIPATION IN JESUS CHRIST

While John proclaims that trusting in Jesus is life in Jesus's name, Paul takes this a step further in that faith/trust is participation in the death and resurrection of Christ.[48] Faith as trust is the mystical means by which the believer/truster participates in Christ's life—that is, the life of the Trustee.[49] Consider Paul's Epistle to the Galatians: "I have been crucified with Christ; it is no longer I who live, but Christ who lives in me; and the life I now live in the flesh I live by [*trust*] in the Son of God, who loved me and gave himself for me" (Gal 2:20 RSV).

The mystery of faith in Jesus Christ is that trusting in Jesus is participation in Jesus's incarnation, death, and resurrection—Jesus dwelling in the person's heart through faith (Eph 3:17). This is the new creation that reconciles the whole of the person, including the imagination, to Christ. Indeed, it is quite possible only through the reconciled imagination to grab hold of the promise that the believer through baptism has already died with Christ and has been raised

---

48 There are many voices contributing to the question of the place of faith/trust in Paul's writings. Of these, consider the fine studies of Gupta and Hagen Pifer: "The point is not works or faith, nor is it faith versus faithfulness. For Paul the gospel does not summon believers either to *beliefs* or to *obedient actions* per se. *Rather*, it is a call for *trust*"; Gupta, *Paul and the Language*, 166. Also "Absolutely essential to this whole process is that salvation by faith is wholly Christological. By faith, the believer is wrapped up in the Christ-mediated process of salvation through identifying with the Christ-event (past), living in a new mode of dependent existence upon a new Lord (present), and living always with hope of being reunited with him in the future. Yet again, faith is absolutely and fundamentally participatory in nature"; Hagen Pifer, *Faith as Participation*, 62.

49 Participation in Christ, referred to variously as *divinization*, *deification*, or *theosis* in Eastern Christianity, has gained traction in recent years in the traditions of the Reformation. The Finnish School of Lutheranism, in part because of living in the confluence of Western and Eastern Christianity, has identified a significant resonance between Luther's theology and deification. Emblematic of the Finnish School is Mannermaa, *Christ Present in Faith*, which explores the real presence of Christ *in faith* (*in ipsa fide Christus adest*) as Luther's paradigm for justification. Lest deification remain an interest only in my dear Lutheran theological ghetto, there is exploration as well as deification in Reformed traditions; cf. Mosser, "Recovering," 3–24.

(Rom 6:4; Col 2:12). Paul writes in 2 Corinthians, "From now on, therefore, we regard no one from a human point of view; even though we once knew Christ from a human point of view, we no longer know him in that way. So if anyone is in Christ, there is a new creation: everything old has passed away; look, new things have come into being!" (2 Cor 5:16–17).

Being in Christ, a synonym for faith, *conforms the imagination to Christ.* If we no longer regard (imagine that!) anyone from a human point of view, we no longer define people by their sin. We see, perceive, imagine in and through Jesus Christ. The imagination, while never fully untethered from the old on this side of the grave, is captive in faith to the new. The new creation remains largely invisible and so is accessible only through the reconciled imagination. The Christian, whose life is "hidden with Christ in God" (Col 3:3), sees in a mirror dimly (1 Cor 13:12) through faith.

CONCLUSION

Faith is trust. Reading πίστις and its Hebrew antecedents as *trust* helps shed light on the essence of this concept central to Christianity in large part because every human being must sort through what it means to trust or not, what it means to be trustworthy or not, every single day of their life. Shifting our language to trust does not make faith simplistic. It does make it real, especially for those outside the church's lexicon.

When we consider the basic trust/trustworthiness relationship equation—X → Y for Z—the human being (X) trusts the Trustworthy One (Y) for Z. So what is Z? For what do we trust in Jesus Christ? In short, life in Jesus's name (John 20:31). This life is characterized by freedom. Not the "Don't Tread on Me" sort of freedom. Rather, freedom from the power and shackles of sin (trusting in that which is not God) and from the power of death.

Grounded in the language of Christian Scripture and tradition, faith as trust opens the horizon of how the Christian participates in the life of God. The triune God, who is trustworthy, invites the human being's trust. Above all else. Trusting in Jesus above all else changes the world in which we live. More accurately, trusting in Jesus reveals the world as it is *in Christ*. This is unreasonable given the shitmess(es) in which we live. The world as it is *in Christ* is only perceptible by way of the reconciled imagination.

CHAPTER THREE

On Imagination

> I am enough of an artist to draw freely upon my imagination. Imagination is more important than knowledge. Knowledge is limited. Imagination encircles the world.
>
> —Albert Einstein, interview in the *Saturday Evening Post*

> The human imagination is one of the last frontiers of the mind.
>
> —Ruth M. J. Byrne, *The Rational Imagination*

Join us on the floor.

When our son, Isaac Oban, was a wee fellow, he began to reeducate me about the importance of imagination. Perhaps you have been invited by a little one into such a space, invited to return to a once familiar land freely accessible as a child but often forgotten amid the demands and distractions of adulthood.

His preferred dominion for play was the floor. Any floor. From a vast floor of an airport gate in Gardermoen, Norway, to the worn and tattered carpet in our tiny flat in St. Andrews, his imagination transformed floors into other worlds. These floors-become-worlds, invisible to me, stretched out around him in every direction. A menagerie of creatures and vehicles were the players in his ever-unfolding drama. The menagerie was most often led by a tiny triumvirate—two visible to all, one only to him: a hard rubber woolly mammoth named Oscar, a tiny yellow creature with pointy ears that he dubbed Funny

Thing, and a completely invisible dog named Licker.[1] (Indeed, Licker pronounced by this three-year-old sounded like "liquor," causing his [still] not altogether mature father to giggle.) These playmates were players in stories that spun out of his imagination. Like a Claymation film without the camera, the menagerie was always on the move through whatever dangers, joys, and challenges lay ahead. To me, this world always looked like a floor. I didn't have his eyes. My imagination was fettered by so-called reality. His imagination was free.

What realms did he explore? What adventures did they have? What problems were created and solved? What tensions drove the plot? I'm not sure, but they were real. For the moment. For the day. Sometimes longer. Oscar, Funny Thing, and Licker led their band of companions on epic adventures. There was dialogue and intrigue. There was good and bad. There was joy and sadness. There were enemies and friends. I was regularly awestruck at this regular transformation of a floor into a whole new world.

This is imagination undiminished by attempts to define it, to pin it down clinically, philosophically, physiologically. Imagination lived. Free. Emergent. Not taught but discovered.

Imagination is a phenomenon not outwardly dependent upon the gospel of Jesus Christ. At the same time, imagination is a fundamental aspect of being human and therefore a gift of God. Imagination, *like trust*, is a phenomenon that can be explored outside the immediate orbit of the church and theological reflection. Imagination is a common denominator of all human beings no matter a person's religious beliefs or affiliations. At the same time, what is at stake is deeply theological. What makes a human being a human being? What does it mean that the human being is created in the image of God (Gen 1:26)? What does it mean that the gospel of Jesus Christ is a narrative that the human being is invited to inhabit? A narrative in which the Christian is invited to recognize not only themselves

---

1 It came to light later that Funny Thing was actually . . . Pikachu of Pokémon fame. No matter, really. Funny Thing was too good to be typecast. He was a character actor with great range in our son's imaginings.

but also and especially their neighbor, their enemy, and the rest of the cosmos?

We humans are fundamentally imaginative beings. Through trusting in Jesus Christ, our imaginations are reconciled to the source of all life, healing, and wholeness: the triune God. This reconciliation of the imagination through trust in the Trustworthy One reveals the world as it is and invites the Christian into a radical freedom to be *in Christ.*

IMAGINATION ENCIRCLES THE WORLD

A few years after being awarded the Nobel Prize in Physics in 1921, Albert Einstein had become enough of a public figure that the *Saturday Evening Post* published a wide-ranging interview with him. This chat happened in Einstein's home over glasses of strawberry juice (Einstein didn't drink alcohol) and seems to have included the famous physicist playing a bit on his beloved violin. The encounter took place between the two world wars of the twentieth century. The optimism of the 1920s would be shattered very soon. The interview was published on Saturday, October 26, 1929. So called Black Tuesday would come to pass three days later, on October 29, 1929. Stock exchanges and monetary systems worldwide crumbled, incubating the conditions for the germination of the Second World War.

Against this backdrop, we receive a gem of insight into imagination. Einstein's theory of general relativity, theoretical physics built upon pure mathematics, had recently been verified experimentally. The interviewer inquired of Einstein, "Do you ascribe your own discoveries to intuition or inspiration?"

> EINSTEIN: I believe in intuitions and inspirations. I sometimes feel that I am right. I do not know that I am. When two expeditions of scientists . . . went forth to test my theory of relativity, I was convinced that their conclusions would tally with my hypothesis. I was not surprised when the

> eclipse of May 29, 1919, confirmed my intuitions. I would have been surprised if I had been wrong.
>
> INTERVIEWER: Then you trust more to your imagination than to your knowledge?
>
> EINSTEIN: I am enough of an artist to draw freely upon my imagination. Imagination is more important than knowledge. Knowledge is limited. Imagination encircles the world.

Just days before the optimism of a generation scarred by trench warfare was to be shattered by more years of hardship and war, there is this little glimmer of light: "Knowledge is limited. Imagination encircles the world."

To say that "imagination encircles the world" bespeaks the power of the imagination. Imagination has great power to open vistas, to invite people to envision what is as yet over the horizon, to be a catalyst for creativity. Imagination, accompanied by wonder and curiosity, can draw us human beings closer to one another and to the creation we share with our neighbor creatures. Imagination's power can also be captured by fear, hate, and shame, whether hate-fueled pseudoscience like Nazi "eugenics" or the fearmongering xenophobia of contemporary Trumpism.

Einstein's musings about his disposition toward discovery capture the beautiful power of imagination. At the same time, the susceptibility of the imagination to wickedness needs to be kept in mind. Hence when exploring the idea of the imagination of faith—that is, the imagination reconciled to God—it is important to be mindful of what the imagination needs to be reconciled from. Building upon the previous chapter, the imagination, if it is to be the imagination of faith, needs to be reconciled from the powers of guilt, shame, fear, and death. All of these are antithetical to—even enemies of[2]—the

2 I am grateful to Jennifer Agee for this insight.

reconciled imagination; imagination *in Christ* encircles the world, *God's good creation*, without partiality.[3]

TO IMAGINE IS TO BE HUMAN

To imagine is to be human. To be human is to be, or at least to have been, a child. To see not only a cardboard box but a hideout. To see not only a bare floor but a whole new world. To see not only a sidewalk but a canvas. To see not only an empty lot but a major-league ballpark. To see what is in front of you not merely as old news but as something potentially wonder filled. A robin's nest woven of delicate branches and laden with turquoise eggs that hold the promise of new life. Likewise, a seed that sprouts and emerges from the soil. A cloud that reveals itself as a dragon flying through the sky. Letters on a page that emerge as poems and stories that open new worlds. A person who is a sinner seen as a child of God for whom Christ died.

Children are not the only people on the planet that imagine, but they are our teachers. Rachel Carson (1907–64), marine biologist, naturalist, and author, helped nurture the public imagination about the breadth and depth and interdependence of life around us, the webs of flora and fauna that we call nature. In a brief memoir of time spent in nature with her young nephew Roger, she invites her readers to see through a child's eyes:

> A child's world is fresh and new and beautiful, full of wonder and excitement. *It is our misfortune that for most of us that clear-eyed vision, that true instinct for what is beautiful and awe-inspiring, is dimmed and even lost before we reach adulthood.* If I had influence with the good fairy who is supposed to preside over the christening of all children, I should ask that her gift to each child in the world be a sense of wonder so

---

3 Scripture is clear that while human beings consistently demonstrate a capacity for partiality of all kinds, there is no partiality in God—e.g., Luke 20:21; Acts 10:34; Rom 2:11; Gal 2:6; Jas 2:9.

> indestructible that it would last throughout life, as an unfailing antidote against the boredom and disenchantments of later years, the sterile preoccupation with things that are artificial, the alienation from the sources of our strength.[4]

Carson invites us to recognize what is lost but also to envision what is possible when the imagination is nurtured and sustained. Some may say that it is inevitable, even natural, as we age and grow, as our minds are stretched and horizons broadened, that our imagination dulls and our sense of wonder diminishes. Things become old hat. Whatever the cause or the inevitability, Carson is spot-on that this is "our misfortune." Perhaps the misfortune is simply the cataracts of maturity and there is a way to mitigate this loss with a kind of cataract surgery of the soul.

How might we see the world through the eyes that are caught up by wonder? How might children become our teachers? How might we recover wonder about the world, about relationships, about ourselves that skepticism (even cynicism) has dimmed? These are big questions that this book pokes at—both generally and from the standpoint of Christian wonder—as we move toward the imagination of faith. Before we get there, it is important to have at least a bit of an understanding of what imagination is.

CONSIDERING IMAGINATION

A bit like *faith*, *imagination* is an oft-used, malleable word that can be both vapid and meaningful. It is a word that we regularly use with confidence. Whether positive ("Her writing is rich with imagination") or negative ("That boy has such an overactive imagination"), imagination falls into the category of the duck: if it walks like a duck and talks like a duck, it is likely a duck. And though there are a whole variety of ducks, we know one when we see one.

---

4 Carson, *Sense of Wonder*, 44 (emphasis added).

A basic upside of a collective ascent to a common definition of any word is that when we humans share the same understanding, language can serve as a bridge. Theologian David Tracy says that we belong to our language far more than it belongs to us.[5] We are most free to be together, to commune with one another, within a common language. A common language with shared definitions does not guarantee harmony and peace. Community within language takes constant tending, and it requires conversation, questioning, and occasional argument. Common language enables us to be together, to share ideas, to share ourselves, if only imperfectly and in part. Common language enables dialogue and community.[6]

A downside of definition is that it can have the capacity to squeeze the mystery out of something, perhaps most especially within the academy or within the Google Translate bot. In terms of defining imagination, it is a duck. We know it when we see it . . . at least most of the time. A child with a floor. A painter with her canvas. Einstein playing with his equations. Yo-Yo Ma facilitating a global musical soundscape with the Silkroad Ensemble.[7] Gratefully, we have fellow creatures among us called poets who play with words in ways that draw the reader to the edges of polyvalence and mystery without killing the duck.

With both upsides and downsides in mind, one must meander around the idea of imagination with a wide radius to see it as fully as possible in all its complexity, not unlike the meander around faith and trust in the previous chapter. For the sake of brevity, consider five primary aspects of imagination. Imagination

1. makes present that which is not;
2. recalls and stitches together the fragments of experience (memories) that compose a person's life story;

5 Tracy, *Plurality and Ambiguity.*

6 Similarly, "Because being-together, as an existential condition for the possibility of any dialogical structure of discourse, appears as a way of trespassing or overcoming the fundamental solitude of each human being"; Ricoeur, *Interpretation Theory*, 15.

7 See Silkroad Ensemble, https://www.silkroad.org.

3. supposes a future, even multiple futures;
4. can create that which does not have an analogy in our experience of the physical world; and
5. can create that which did not exist before.[8]

Were this book only about imagination, it would be important to push through the full range of these facets.[9] For our purposes, however, the range is limited by space, time, and intention, as the goal of this book is to see the interrelatedness of faith, imagination, and freedom.

I want to suggest a simpler definition. A friend and scholar of the imagination, Jennifer Agee,[10] suggested to me that perhaps imagination is the capacity to see "creative connections"[11] among things, ideas, memories, experiences. There is a beauty in such a definition, especially as a complement to the previous range of the imagination's facets.

LANGUAGE AND IMAGINATION

Humans are imaginative beings insofar as we have the innate capacity to make creative connections. While we are not alone in this (e.g., our mammalian cousin the rat has a basic capacity to imagine[12]), in our immediate corner of the cosmos, it seems that we are the creatures able to develop, reflect collectively upon, and direct our imaginations.

On a very basic level, we are "languaged" creatures. We live within language. We interpret the world through language. Drawing again upon the observations of David Tracy, "Language is not

8 These five facets of imagination are paraphrased from the *Oxford English Dictionary*, ad loc.

9 Philosophers for ages and more recently psychologists and neurobiologists have dug deeply into the imagination.

10 Agee, *Systematic Mythology*.

11 Cf. Agee's poem, "Eriosomatinae," forthcoming, which explores the wonder and imagination by way of considering the woolly aphid.

12 Davies, *Imagination*, 267.

an instrument that I can pick up and put down at will; it is always already there, surrounding and invading all I experience, understand, judge, decide, and act upon. I belong to my language far more than it belongs to me, and through that language I find myself participating in this particular history and society."[13] Language is the matrix within which we share life and ideas with one another, by which we reason and imagine. Hans-Georg Gadamer puts it succinctly: "Being that can be understood is language."[14] Essential to our being is the language(s) in which we swim. So we ponder the water.

The basic building block of language is the word, a collection of sounds that when arranged in a particular way represents something, such as a thing, an action, an idea.[15] The word is a—perhaps *the*—basic exercise of the imagination. With a few exceptions, such as the word *word*, which is what it represents, words represent what they are not. The word *dog*, for example, is not itself a four-legged furry creature fond of sniffing the butts of other creatures as a way of saying, "Hi. How are you? Where have you been? What did you have for breakfast?" The word *dog* represents the creature without being the creature. Whenever it was that you learned to associate the word *dog* (maybe at first *doggy*) with the furry creature that licked your face, pooped in the yard, and slept at the end of the bed, this was a basic exercise of the imagination. It was unnecessary for your father or mother to explain to you that the word *dog* is an abstract representation of *Canis familiaris*, the common dog, which was at some point domesticated from the wolf and now exists in a host of

13 Tracy, *Plurality and Ambiguity*, 49–50.

14 Gadamer, *Truth and Method*, 489.

15 Not to undermine the place of the word as the smallest kernel of the imaginative nature of the human being, but it is important to recall with Paul Ricoeur that the sentence is the most basic building block of discourse, as it is in the context of a sentence that the word's meaning takes on a fuller communicative function of referring beyond itself: "In the system of language, say as a lexicon, there is no problem with reference; signs only refer to other signs within the system. With the sentence, however, language is directed beyond itself. Whereas the sense is immanent to the discourse, and objective in the sense of the ideal, the reference expresses the movement in which language transcends itself"; Ricoeur, *Interpretation Theory*, 20.

individual breeds as well as in innumerable variations of the Heinz 57 neighborhood special. Rather, in the movement of language acquisition, someone probably pointed to a furry friend and said something like, "Look at the doggy. Can you say *doggy*?" And boom, you learned to creatively connect the furry creature with the three-letter, one-syllable word *dog*.

How humans acquire language is a complex process that is deeply abstract in concept but equally practical in application—a complex mixture of nature and nurture.[16] When, for example, we learn to associate the word *apple* with a piece of fruit, it is not long thereafter that we begin to distinguish between apples and kiwis, between one apple and three apples, between red apples and green apples. In this exercise of association, our brains are formed to note that stuff can be referenced with words, a particular organization of sounds that in yet another level of abstraction we eventually associate with words on a page. All the while, the word *apple* is an abstraction. With this great power of imagination, we can also draw a picture of an apple and call the image an apple as well. As we acquire language, our imaginative capacity grows from the kernel word that has a physical referent to far more abstract, imaginatively complex movements, like friend and enemy, war and peace, life and death.

When we begin to think about imagination as an aspect—*a central aspect*—of what makes a human being a human being, this might appear as a domestication of the imagination. Consider that we often associate imagination with great works of art or literature or music. Many folks, in their appreciation of the great works, also hear a tiny but persistent voice that says, "You can't do that. So why try?" Or "You're not creative." Or "You don't have the imagination for . . ." One benefit of recognizing the *quotidian* nature of the imagination is that all human beings have it. Of course, given that we are all wired and experienced differently with varied passions and pursuits, this is not going to have any kind of substantive uniformity *except* that we

16 In truth, language acquisition is more complex and debated than this paragraph infers. Cf. Ambridge and Lieven, *Child Language Acquisition*, especially chap. 3.

all have this innate imagination that is essential for navigating life and the world and for understanding who we are. Sometimes, this quotidian imagination squirts out sideways, yielding a masterpiece of art or literature or music.[17]

METAPHOR AND IMAGINATION

Metaphor may be the prime example of how language forms the human imagination. The philosopher Paul Ricoeur argues that metaphor is a juxtaposition of two dissimilar things in a kind of "calculated error." Out of the tension of the calculated error, something new emerges: "What is at stake in a metaphorical utterance . . . is the appearance of kinship where ordinary vision does not perceive any relationship. . . . It is, in effect, a calculated error, which brings together things that do not go together and by means of this apparent misunderstanding it causes a new, hitherto unnoticed, relation

17 Consider the following: "This ability to conjure up images, ideas, impressions, intentions and the like: This is the imagination at work. The conceptual space it spans is stupendously vast, stretching across the real and the unreal, the possible and the impossible. Its workings are spontaneous and deliberate, ordinary and extraordinary, conscious and unconscious, deriving from the outer world external to our bodies as well as our inner world. The word 'imagination' is therefore a particularly curious one. Because if 'words are really the history of people's agreement about things' [Edwin Schlossberg speaking with Debbie Millman on the *Design Matters* podcast on March 5, 2018], then what we apparently agree on is that this word is one that can be imbued with an exuberance of disparate meanings that emerge from across the incalculable breadth and depth of human experience that constitutes our mental lives. A key point to note right at the outset is that 'we use imagination in our ordinary perception of the world. This perception cannot be separated from interpretation. Interpretation can be common to everyone, and in this sense ordinary, or it can be inventive, personal and revolutionary. . . . So imagination is necessary to enable us to recognize things in the world as familiar. . . . But it is also necessary if we are to see the world as significant of something unfamiliar'"; Abraham, "Surveying the Imagination Landscape," 1. The reference for Abraham's final quote is Warnock, *Imagination*, 10.

of meaning to spring up between the terms that previous systems of classification had ignored or not allowed."[18]

A child's initial acquisition of the word *apple* likely results from a direct, material connection to a piece of fruit, perhaps red, perhaps green, that grew on an apple tree (*Malus domestica*), whose juicy flesh is both sweet and tart. Like a duck is a duck, an apple is an apple. The word *apple* is not itself an apple but represents one. But when you say to someone, "You are the apple of my eye," you are employing Ricoeur's calculated error. Is the person about whom you are swooning really a piece of fruit from an apple tree? No. Metaphor (from the Greek μετά/across and φέρω/carry) results in an unnatural bridge. In this case, I am holding "you" in creative tension with a lovely, sweet piece of fruit. By way of this calculated error, I am imagining into being an understanding that would not exist without the calculated error.

With the introduction of metaphors into the language, the imagination is further formed and practiced. We learn early in the acquisition of language that two things that do not obviously or logically go together can be placed next to each other in ways that yield new meaning or insight. In Ricoeur's words, metaphors "tell us something new about reality."[19] Metaphors are fundamentally imaginative, especially insofar as they employ creative connections, imaginative juxtapositions that tell or show us something new.

FLESHY IMAGINATION

Is imagination, however, merely a linguistic phenomenon? How does it relate to our corporeal, bodily reality? As a former student once said to me, we humans are meat sacks.[20] We are flesh-and-blood creatures made up of a variety of cells powered by energy that originated in

18 Ricoeur, *Interpretation Theory*, 51.

19 Ricoeur, *Interpretation Theory*, 53.

20 My gratitude goes to former student Cassandra Borges for introducing me to this poetic, anthropological flourish.

the star at the center of our galaxy, echoing from the creation of the cosmos some 13.8 billion years ago.

We are embodied—our minds as much as our hearts and hands and feet. When we imagine something, just like when our brains are active in other ways, neurons are firing.[21] Imagination is corporeal. Physical. But the how of imagination remains somewhat unclear. Cognitive scientist Ruth Byrne reports that "the human imagination is one of the last frontiers of the mind."[22] Cue the opening to *Star Trek*! This is not to say that neuroscience has not made great strides in understanding the corporeal workings of the brain that relate to imagination. Rather, as with so many questions about the brain, the mind, and the basic notion of what it means to be human, there remains a host of questions to be explored. These questions will not be answered here.[23] The point, rather, is that *to imagine is to be human.* We are corporeally hardwired to hold the world together with stories and images. Psychologist Arnold Modell observes, "What is uniquely human is a generative imagination from which the individual can create an internal unseen world."[24] The imagination plays a critical role in how the human negotiates life, organizes memory, experiences meaning or meaninglessness, and envisions a future. The internal, unseen world has much to do with how we interpret and negotiate the external, seen one.

DUELING WITH DESCARTES

In 1637, mathematician and philosopher René Descartes (1596–1650) penned the words *Cogito ergo sum*—"I think, therefore I am."[25] Descartes's impact on how people think about imagination appeared (at

21 Davies, *Imagination*, 1.

22 Byrne, *Rational Imagination*, 197.

23 For a much fuller exploration, cf. Erickson, *Imagination in the Western Psyche*.

24 Modell, *Imagination and the Meaningful Brain*, 33.

25 In a recent translation, Ian MacLean proposes a more dynamic translation: "I am thinking, therefore I am"; cf. Descartes, *Discourse on the Method*, 28.

least in part) via the bifurcation of mind and body: *I think*, therefore I am. The focus is on the mind. Emblematic of Enlightenment optimism about the power of reason, Descartes's theory of correspondence suggested that ideas are pure and directly represent or correspond to their object, that which exists in the real world. When the idea of an apple represents an apple, the idea is true. The idea and the thing correspond. With such correspondence, the thinking of the mind could be represented with mathematical precision divorced from the influence of emotion or passion.[26]

The fixation on pure reason by Descartes and others has had the legacy of elevating reason to unreasonable (Apologies. Pun intended!) and idealistic heights. While Descartes's theory of correspondence has fallen from grace, his elevation of reason has remained. An effect of this has been that imagination has had to play—*at best*—second or third fiddle. Imagination is flimsy, lacking a concrete connection to the real world.[27] The mind, properly working, reasons the truths of the world and can therefore be objective. Information gathered from imagination or gleaned by the senses was less true than the yield of reason. Consider a brief excerpt from Descartes's *Discourse on the Method*, wherein he discusses the acquisition of knowledge in relation to the existence of the human being and of God:

> What convinces many people that there is a problem in knowing [God] and even of knowing what their soul is, is that they never raise their mind above the realm of sensory things and are so used not to thinking of anything except by imagining it, which is a mode of thinking peculiar to material objects, that everything which seems unimaginable seems to them

26 Modell, *Imagination and the Meaningful Brain*, 6.

27 Kind and Kung, in "The Puzzle of the Imaginative Use," 6, describe Descartes's disposition toward the imagination as "pessimistic," continuing, "Like other rationalists, Descartes dismisses imagination as the wrong kind of faculty to produce the secure knowledge that he seeks. Instead, he settles on clear and distinct perception—what we might now be more inclined to call rational insight—as the principal source of knowledge."

> unintelligible. This is clear enough from the fact that even scholastic philosophers hold as a maxim that there is nothing in the intellect which has not previously been in the senses, in which, however, it is certain that the ideas of God and the soul have never been. It seems to me that people who wish to use their imagination in order to understand these ideas are doing the same as if, in order to hear sounds or smell smells, they tried to use their eyes. Except that there is this further difference, that the sense of sight no more confirms to us the reality of things than that of smell or hearing, whereas neither our imagination nor our senses could ever confirm the existence of anything, if our intellect did not play its part.[28]

Descartes's elevation of reason and his diminishment of other epistemological equipment are clear here. Experience (the senses) and imagination come in a distant second to reason. Imagination is not as reliable.

In contrast to this and at the risk of oversimplification, contemporary neuroscience's exploration of how the human being navigates and makes sense of the world might be pushing toward a description of the human being: *I imagine, therefore I am*. The sexier Latin (yes, this is an academic's bias): *Imaginor, ergo sum*.

In the late 1990s, two Italian scientists, Vittorio Gallese and Giacomo Rizzolatti, identified something within the physiology of the brains of primates (including us humans) called "mirror neurons." Through a series of behavioral experiments, the work determined that "when mirror neurons are activated, there is a very tight, precise correspondence between specific motor actions and neuron firing. For example, if a neuron responded to an object held between the fingers, it would not respond to the same object held by tweezers. Self-initiated actions and the individual's perception of the identical action performed by another evoke the same neural response."[29] The key bit discerned by our Italian friends that impacts this current

28 Descartes, *Discourse on the Method*, 32.

29 Modell, *Imagination and the Meaningful Brain*, 184.

exploration is that "this observer/execution matching system provides a bridge from doing to communicating."[30] A theory that flows from this discovery confirms the hypothesis of Giambattista Vico (1668–1744) that prior to the development of language as we know it, our ancestors communicated by metaphoric gestures. The discovery of mirror neurons provides a scientific validation of such a hypothesis. As Modell interprets, "A species that had the capacity for forming conceptual and perceptual metaphors would have expanded its ability for thought exponentially, even though its aptitude for spoken language may have been rudimentary."[31]

Rather beautifully, Modell concludes that this metaphorical capacity is imagination hardwired into our brains by way of mirror neurons. As such, we have the capacity to communicate with gestures and with dance, a common denominator across cultures.[32] This suggests that within an evolutionary scope of development, imagination might well precede the development of language. Given the discovery of the mirror neuron, which provides a basic capacity to communicate by means of metaphoric gestures that necessitate imagination, it might be more accurate to say, *I imagine, therefore I am*. This is not, of course, to say that reason is unimportant. Reason helps sort out what is imagined, but imagination may well precede reason and, I dare say, form reason.

---

30 Rizzolatti and Arbib, "Language within Our Grasp," 188, quoted in Modell, *Imagination and the Meaningful Brain*, 184.

31 Modell, *Imagination and the Meaningful Brain*, 189.

32 Another observation that Modell makes about the emerging data around mirror neurons is that human beings are also hardwired for relationships: "The discovery of mirror neurons suggests that certain actions may be represented in the mind because they trigger a neural link between the self and other. This representation of the other's actions by means of mirror neurons is direct and immediate and does not require any intervening symbolic code or a mental language, as there is an instantaneous mapping from self to other and from other to self. Mirror neurons support ecological theories of perception in that there is an innate coupling between the self and the other: we respond to directly perceived qualities of the other's intentionality; we do not require coded information"; Modell, 185. This relational wiring, together with the metaphorical gesture/dance, will return when the imagination and freedom are explored within the orbit of liturgy.

To summarize this little duel with Descartes while awkwardly holding hands with neuroscience, we human beings are hardwired for imagination in such a deep way that it is likely that imagination has developmental priority over reason. We navigate the world; we become human by means of narrative and images that flow from our capacity to imagine. Even before we know how to associate a spoken or written word with that which it represents—recall dogs and apples—we have been hardwired to interpret the metaphorical gesture, the sacred dance.

IMAGINATION'S POWER

Recall again Einstein's remark: "I am enough of an artist to draw freely upon my imagination. Imagination is more important than knowledge. Knowledge is limited. Imagination encircles the world." In no way was he devaluing reason. On the contrary, what he was doing was recognizing the primary place of imagination in discovery. Imagination is the capacity to envision creative, metaphoric connections. Imagination frees the individual from the constraints or limitations of knowledge, which, whether in science or theology, is always penultimate at best, "relatively adequate," à la David Tracy.[33] Discovery is about the future moving toward the present. Imagination can remove cataracts that blur our vision of what is and of what is possible.

Imagination frees us from only seeing what is. From what we have been conditioned to think is. From what is familiar. Reality is always plural. Something is what it is, but it is also simultaneously what it was and what it might be. Imagination frees us to sort through aspects of the world in search of meaning, in pursuit of truth.

Herein lies the often-uneasy relationship between science and religion. For many, it is important to note, there is no problem. There are many pious Christian folks, among whom I find myself, for whom the

33 Tracy, *Plurality and Ambiguity*, 22–23.

epistemologies of science and religion are complementary. As with so many things, however, the squeaky wheel gets the grease. This is not the venue for wading into the swamp of the contemporary miss of science and Christianity, other than to say that both science and religion depend on imagination. That is, both require an openness to that which is not yet—to connections yet to be made.

In a popular 2007 study of how certain artists have envisioned advancements in neuroscience prior to scientists, Jonah Lehrer demonstrates how the imaginations of the likes of Walt Whitman, Marcel Proust, and Virginia Woolf saw beyond the horizons of what science knew at the time.[34] Science and art both pursue truth, albeit within different epistemological matrices. Lehrer explores examples of the symbiosis of science and art. Of the project, he writes, "We are made of art and science. We are such stuff as dreams are made on, but we are also just stuff. . . . Science needs art to frame the mystery, but art needs science so that not everything is a mystery. Neither truth alone is our solution, for our reality exists in plural."[35] Art and religion are not the same thing, yet religion shares the qualities of art more than the qualities of science. What Lehrer says of art functions also for theology, as theology's pursuit of truth is not empirical but creative, artistic, interpretive. It is mythopoesis.

"Every brilliant experiment, like every great work of art, starts with an act of imagination."[36] In addition, every act of imagination is an act of freedom—freedom to see and to explore that which is yet invisible. Physicist and writer Alan Lightman adds, "Just as the world needs both certainty and uncertainty, the world needs questions with answers and questions without answers."[37] We human beings are imaginative creatures, and imagination yields both a sense of wonder for wonder's sake and a sense of wonder for the sake of discovery. We are wired to sit in awe at the slow, deliberate movement of a woolly bear caterpillar (a.k.a. *Pyrrharctia isabella*, which

---

34 Lehrer, *Proust Was a Neuroscientist.*

35 Lehrer, x.

36 Lehrer, x.

37 Lightman, *Sense of the Mysterious*, 19.

eventually emerges as an isabella tiger moth) across a dirt path on a warm fall day, and we are wired to try to understand this fellow inhabitant of Earth. Such wondering might include the basic question born of a recognition that our knowledge is always penultimate: What makes that little bugger tick?

Imagination is naturally accompanied by the likes of wonder, play, and creativity. This is true even if we figure into the claim a corrective to help avoid mere nostalgia. Imagination frees the person for wonder and discovery because it can transform calcified knowledge into malleable knowledge. Categorizing knowledge as penultimate or "relatively adequate"[38] means that what is known is always available for further questions and exploration. Such acknowledgment of the penultimate nature of knowledge is freedom. Imagination frees the person for both wonder and discovery. Wonder because the universe is not limited to old news. Discovery as imagination can travel in realms as yet unexplored in search of creative connections as yet unseen.

Consider for a moment the work of contemporary theoretical physics, in particular the striving for the so-called theory of everything, which, if discovered, would hold together the truths of general relativity and quantum mechanics. The measurements associated with the smallest units of length and time that the granularity of our physical reality will sustain are Planck length (10^{-33} centimeters) and Planck time (10^{-44} seconds).[39] Theoretically, in a vacuum, it takes light one unit of Planck time to travel one Plank length. I say "theoretically," as there are no instruments available today that are capable of measuring such extremely tiny things. From the realm of quantum mechanics, everything—absolutely everything—is composed of these exponentially minute bits and bobs, which are always on the move and always exist in relation to other bits and bobs. As such, theoretical physicist Carlo Rovelli says, "The world is not a collection of things, it is a collection of events,"[40] these quantum-level interactions. These tiny building blocks of the cosmos, of you and

38 See Tracy, *Plurality and Ambiguity*, 22–23.

39 Named for renowned German physicist Max Planck (1858–1947).

40 Rovelli, *Order of Time*, 96.

me and everyone and everything else, are only imaginable. At the same time, they are no less real.

Similarly but in the opposite order of magnitude, the distance from Earth to Proxima Centauri, the closest star to the big ball of fire that we on Earth travel around and call the sun, is 4.24 light-years. When we catch a glimpse in the night sky of this closest neighbor, what we are seeing is the light that left that star four and a quarter years ago. We cannot see it in a now that is equivalent to our now on Earth. When we see it now, we are looking more than a presidential election cycle (US reference) into the past. This distance—4.24 light-years—is nearly 2.5×10^{13} miles. Just as Planck measurements are mindblowers to imagine on the tiny side of things, so too is the distance even to our closest neighboring star—that distance is like going between Earth and the sun 264,768 times. Each leg of the journey would cover 94.14 million miles. That's 2.11×10^{11} steps, give or take. Roughly 211 trillion steps. Each way. Your pedometer might have just exploded at the mere possibility.

So here we sit. Human beings with an average life expectancy on planet Earth of about seventy years, an average height of around 165 cm / 5′5″. How do we even begin to imagine hanging around with the tiniest components of the physical world and wandering into the wider cosmos? We are simultaneously giants and gnats. What does it mean to be a lowly human being in a cosmos of such extremes?[41] Extremes from a human point of view, that is. From the standpoint of the imagination, consider that at least one thing that this means is that the world is always bigger and smaller than we can experience.

NURTURING WONDER

Like both reason and the glutes, imagination needs to be exercised, worked, developed, questioned, nurtured. And like reason and the glutes, if not nurtured, imagination—and with it, wonder—atrophies.

41 Consider what Rudolf Otto called "creature feeling"; Otto, *Idea of the Holy*, 8–11.

One of the things that we adults do to so many of the wonder-filled wee ones among us is to disembowel their imaginations and step on their sense of wonder. We squish out of them this natural sense of wonder and awe that fuels curiosity and serves as fodder for the imagination. In the name of growing up ("adulting," as our dear daughter calls it), we domesticate their imaginations. Wolves are dangerous; lapdogs, not so much. From the time of childhood, we teach our wild, ravenous imagination to do a few tricks and spend most of its life asleep in the sun as if the world we inhabit is dull and colorless. As if our knowledge is ultimate. As if life is wonderless.

As an educator, I see it. I do it. It has been done to me, this domestication. I trust that it has been done to you as well. We have all heard of lesson plans with the objective of coaxing the child to color inside the lines. We have heard it because it is true. We work very hard as a society, as adults, as parents to domesticate our children. We work diligently to turn them from wild-minded little creatures who play in the mud, chase grasshoppers, and transform the floor into a wonder-filled realm into productive members of society who conform to civil predictability *for their own good, for ours, and for the good of civil society.* We work hard at getting that kid to color inside the lines.

A certain amount of domestication is necessary. For all kinds of reasons. Much of what we teach our children as they grow is helpful and good as they learn to navigate a world that can be cruel and deceiving. It is important that the child matures, gains independence, and has a sense of agency in a world that has the capacity and the drive to consume them. It is critical that parents teach the dance of increased independence and responsibility for many reasons, from the perpetuation of the species; to the child developing their own sense of self, disentangled from their parents; to looking both ways before crossing the street.

But we do our children a disservice in the arena of wonder and imagination. In the name of necessary maturation, we kill wonder with worksheets. We stomp out curiosity by Velcroing their butts to desks in nice, neat rows for hours at a time. We unplug them from many of the wonders that are all around. In the name of efficiency and conformity, we regularly sacrifice wonder and imagination on the altars of conformity and predictability.

Perhaps an even greater disservice is to adults. Shouldn't wonder last a lifetime? Isn't this cosmos we inhabit worthy of our curiosity? Einstein was not reminiscing about childhood when he said that imagination encircles the world. He was speaking of the world as the playground of the mind, with imagination drawing the person more deeply into the mysteries and challenges that are all around us.

Rachel Carson penned several books that raised questions about the sustainability of our industrial and agricultural practices of the 1950s and 1960s. Through her scientific work and her appreciation of the power of imagination, she impacted the imagination of the masses regarding the interdependence of the species on the big blue marble.[42] As her research opened her eyes to the sprawling impact of industrialization, she employed her curiosity and pathos about the world around her in ways that helped many reimagine the human being's relationship with the rest of the natural world.

Carson invites her reader to reconnect or remain connected with the ground (literally and metaphorically) of their being. What she does simply and beautifully is to remind us of our interconnectedness with the rest of the world. We do not, in fact, lord over the world to use and abuse however we like. Rather, we exist together with ferns and frogs and hackberry trees in a state of interdependence. Our ability to wonder is a great power that can be directed to help us observe and feel this interconnectedness, or it can be channeled toward more nefarious pursuits, such as imagining the environment we inhabit or the people around us as mere resources to exploit for our benefit.

This is an important distinction to be made. The human imagination is not something that always works for good. While I started

---

42 It is, of course, anachronistic to utter "big blue marble" in relation to Rachel Carson. She died in 1964, and it wasn't until the Apollo 17 mission in 1972 that "big blue marble" made its way into modern parlance. Consider this poetic license, or perhaps prophetic license, in that Carson envisioned the essence of "big blue marble" before it was observed with human eyes.

this chapter by reflecting on a child's imagination, imagination is not immune from humanity's penchant for power, control, dominance, and turning toward theological idolatry (trusting in that which is not God).[43]

I-THOU AND WONDER

A sense of wonder is what draws us human beings into a more intimate relationship with one another and the world around us. A critical dynamic of Carson's beautiful observation about the place of wonder draws us back further in the twentieth century to the work of Martin Buber.

Recall how Buber's *Ich und Du* (*I and Thou*)[44] drew upon two basic relationships: I-It and I-Thou. A quick summary of a couple of Buber's key insights: First, human beings are creatures that exist in relationship. The purely autonomous self is a falsehood. We are who we are in relationship with others. "Others" here can mean other people, your dog, the sugar maple tree in the park, the bald eagles that nest along the river, that woolly bear caterpillar, the ground beneath our feet, our neighbor, or our enemy. We humans are fundamentally relational creatures. It is important to note here that we humans don't have a corner on being relational. Recall the observation about the quantum workings of the cosmos. The more that our sense of curiosity and wonder draws us into the worlds of our fellow creatures, the more it becomes apparent that all creatures are relational. Bees dance for one another. Elephants have death rituals. Whales sing to one another across hundreds of miles of ocean. Recent research even suggests the possibility that trees communicate with one another through subterranean networks of fungi.[45] We humans, perhaps with all our fellow creatures, large and small, are fundamentally wired to be in relationship.

---

43 In chapter 4, I explore the failure of imagination.

44 Buber, *I and Thou*.

45 Simard et al., "Mycorrhizal Networks," 39–60.

Second, Buber observes that we live in two basic kinds of relationships: the I-It and the I-Thou.[46] The basic idea of the I-It is that the other (whatever/whoever the "It" is) is a means to an end. The primary interest of the "I" in the I-It relationship is not the other but what the other can provide. The second relationship is I-Thou or I-You. The difference here is that the interest of the "I" in the I-Thou is the "Thou." Thou is not a means to an end, but the relationship is itself the end, the completion, the telos. While the I-It is characterized by commodification and use, the characteristics of the I-Thou are delight and wonder.[47]

Wonder is more than interest. A person can be interested in something without being drawn to the thing for the thing's sake. Interest is more naturally I-It and wonder more I-Thou. Curiosity is also not the same thing as wonder. Curiosity is a characteristic of the person. A person can exercise their curiosity in either relationship, I-It or I-Thou. Wonder, on the other hand, is the result of being drawn into relationship with Thou.[48] As Buber himself says of the two words,

> The basic word I-[Thou] can only be spoken with one's whole being.
> The basic word I-It can never be spoken with one's whole being.[49]

Wonder involves the whole self in relation.

---

46 Buber speaks of these two relationships as the two basic "words" that the human being can speak, words that "establish a mode of existence"; Buber, *I and Thou*, 53.

47 "Whoever says [Thou] does not have something; he has nothing. But he stands in relation"; Buber, 54.

48 "Wonder prompts us to consider how particularly vivid displays of vitality, beauty, or power might reveal a purpose or intentionality of the universe as a whole. As such, wonder stimulates efforts to discern what is of intrinsic value or meaning (as opposed to what is of utilitarian value or meaning). And it consequently elicits efforts to find a harmonious relationship with, rather than active mastery of, our wider surroundings"; Fuller, *Wonder*, 9.

49 Buber, *I and Thou*, 53.

To be clear, neither interest nor curiosity is by nature bad. Indeed, neither is the I-It relationship bad by nature. It seems quite impossible for any human being to be only in I-Thou relationships or to have the I-Thou relationship never vacillate to reflect at least the dynamics of I-It from time to time.

Bringing this back to the theological, the I-It is more akin to idolatry (trusting in that which is not God), and the I-Thou is more akin to faith (trusting in Jesus Christ).[50] In the I-It, I seek something outside of or beyond the It. Whereas the I-Thou is a holistic encounter. Buber himself wrote of this theological aspect as the Eternal Thou, insofar as "extended, the lines of relationships intersect in the eternal You."[51] There is a holiness to all true wonder in all true I-Thou moments and relationships. Wonder, whether scientific, mystical, or both, is a glimpse of the Eternal Thou. When we take Buber's philosophical and religious observations about the nature of human relationship, which Buber himself extends to the theological, it is important to recall that he was an Orthodox Jew. Approaching his classic observations from the vantage of wonder and imagination, the next natural move for this argument, which is a Christian theological exercise, is the incarnation of Jesus Christ, as it is *in Christ Jesus*—that is, trusting in Christ Jesus—that the person is freed from seeking and freed for seeing the world as it is and for life.

---

50 Theology matters. Bad theology can be destructive. It is quite possible to make an idol of God within the context of a Christian congregation. Consider the creed of moral therapeutic deism, a phenomenon rife with Christian churches across North America: A God exists who created and orders the world and watches over human life on earth. God wants people to be good, nice, and fair to one another, as taught in the Bible and by most world religions. The central goal of life is to be happy and to feel good about oneself. God does not need to be particularly involved in one's life except when God is needed to resolve a problem. Good people go to heaven when they die. Paraphrased from Smith and Denton, *Soul Searching*, 162.

51 Buber, *I and Thou*, 123.

CONCLUSION

Einstein's observation that imagination encircles the world is a helpful vision of the imagination of faith, the imagination reconciled *in Christ.*

We human beings are created as imaginative beings, perhaps even *Imaginor, ergo sum.* From even before the acquisition of language, we are hardwired toward imagination. One need not bring imagination into the orbit of theology, but imagination is deeply theological. If we are indeed created in the image of God (Gen 1:26), then the human imagination is rooted in God's own creative and redeeming disposition toward creation. Like the rest of us humanoids, however, the imagination is in need of being reconciled to its source and ground—the triune God. This reconciliation happens in and through Jesus Christ, and we participate in this reconciliation by trusting in Jesus Christ as Lord and Savior. As the imagination's life in the world, the sense of wonder is akin to trust in Jesus Christ, to faith.

CHAPTER FOUR

The Imagination of Faith

> No matter how much experience we may gather in life, we can never in life get the dimension of experience that the imagination gives us.
>
> —Northrop Frye, *The Educated Imagination*

> The first task of Christian theology in a post-Christian age must be to take leave of the imagination-versus-reality way of thinking once and for all.
>
> —Garrett Green, *Imagining Theology*

There is a poetic encounter in the middle of Psalm 85 that leads to a cosmic kiss, an oh-so-delicate kiss. The moment passes quickly like the beat of a dragonfly's wings. This kiss is the fullness of the imagination of faith. The whole of salvation history in an economy of words sealed with simplicity and beauty:

> Steadfast love and faithfulness will meet;
> righteousness and peace will kiss each other.
> Faithfulness will spring up from the ground,
> and righteousness will look down from the sky.
> (Ps 85:10–11 RSV)[1]

---

1 The biblical backbone of the film *Babette's Feast* (Gabriel Axel, 1987) is Ps 85:10. Cf. Giere, "*Babette's Feast* (1987)," 18–24.

Such a vision is only accessible by means of the imagination of faith. When Jesus says, as he repeatedly does, the kingdom of God/heaven is near, I imagine that this is what he intends. This is the vision. It is something that is only accessible via the aesthetic. The truth here is not rational but poetic. The truth of this eschatological fulfillment of God's reconciling movement toward God's good creation is accessible via the imagination of faith.

REIMAGINING TRUST IN JESUS CHRIST

Rediscovering the centrality of faith in Jesus Christ and with it the imagination of faith is one of the great challenges before the church today. In short, the church is in danger of losing its central focus—its raison d'être, if you will. Of course, the church is not and will never be without Jesus by the power of the Spirit, as the church cannot exist without Christ, its head.[2] The problem, rather, is that we Christians seem keen to displace Christ as Lord and Savior as we search for something "better." That which is better can be anything, but these anythings all boil down to displacing God with ourselves as we seek after and chomp down on the fruit of the tree of the knowledge of good and evil—a faithless generation seeking salvation by a secular theo-ethic. As discussed in chapter 1, during this age *of bad faith*, the object of our trust—this something "better"—is today often an ideology, a system of belief that displaces Jesus with another lord and savior for life, wholeness, or salvation. By pursuing life via an ideology or any other god, we substitute what is death for what is life.

To reiterate, many of these ideologies are well meaning, even noble. From pro-life ideologies that at the core seek to protect the unborn to the contemporary social gospel of inclusivity that seeks to stress that all people, especially those historically excluded and persecuted by church and society, feel welcome, there are well-meaning people who hold these ideologies with the noblest of intentions. The

2 Cf. Ps 118:22; Eph 1:22; Col 1:18.

fundamental problem with these ideologies, as with any ideology, is that the ideology displaces Christ as Lord and Savior with something "better."[3] In doing so, adherents of the ideology, even the noblest, leapfrog over trusting in Jesus as the central means by which the human being participates in the life of the triune God. Because of an ideology's "apparent" goodness, it is difficult to see such systems as gods who demand our trust above all else and by which we draw lines between the righteous and the unrighteous. It is not easy to accept that they are *bad faith* that warps our imagination by conforming our faith to these "noble" objects and objectives.

From the standpoint of imagination, any god that we worship, in whom we put our ultimate trust, warps the narrative in which we live from the gospel of Jesus Christ, who died for sinners, to a gospel of something else. A gospel of anything else draws lines of righteousness and unrighteousness in ways that are incongruent with the gospel of Jesus Christ. Christ died for ungodly sinners, which are us all (Gal 3:21–22; 5:6–8). No exceptions. Faith alone—trusting in Jesus Christ—is *the* means by which the Christian participates in the new creation in Christ. This participation is by way of the reconciliation of the imagination to Christ. That is, in faith in Christ, the Christian's vision of the world is conformed to Christ, becoming the imagination of faith, freeing the person from worshipping other gods. Put positively, the imagination of faith by the power of the Spirit reveals the world in which we live to the world as it is in Christ. As such, the imagination of faith is not a step en route to some holier,

3 Commenting on Gal 2:19–21, "Paul's climactic declaration Χριστῷ συνεσταύρωμαι demonstrates that participation in the Christ-event is a continuous dying to all other systems of lordship within the world and a continuing self-involvement that alters the existence of the believer. . . . Yet, participatory faith does not imply participation in the faith of Christ but rather human dependence upon Christ that is simultaneously self-negating and self-involving because of his efficacious work on the cross and the resulting new life in him. Christ now defines what the believer lives for and by whose power the believer lives because it is by his death that the human is revivified"; Hagen Pifer, *Faith as Participation*, 175.

more perfect, more righteous place; *the imagination of faith is that which the Christian is called to inhabit.*

This chapter articulates the imagination of faith/trust in Jesus Christ. To this point, we have explored the dry rot (a.k.a. the *age of bad faith*, chapter 1), trust/faith (chapter 2), and imagination (chapter 3) as fundamental aspects of being human, thereby accessible to all, whether indoctrinated into the lexicon of the church or not.

From the basic building blocks of language to the power of metaphor, we humans are fundamentally wired to exercise the power of imagination for good or for ill. Imagination has the power to unlock the secrets of a bare floor as an invisible world as well as the power to open the world of quantum mechanics. Einstein's "imagination encircles the world" bespeaks the power of imagination. Like imagination, faith as trust is part and parcel of being human. The Christian is one who has been persuaded by the Holy Spirit through the hearing of the gospel (a.k.a. the trustworthiness of God) to trust in Jesus Christ above all else. This is good faith. Important to remember is that Jesus himself declares what we bring, whether trust in the God of Israel or magical desperation, as faith. Faith/trust conforms to its object, and imagination creates the world in which we live based on this conformation. Hence we consider faith's object: Jesus Christ.

ENVISIONING THE COSMIC CHRIST

If the object of trust is Jesus Christ, then who we understand Jesus Christ to be impacts the formation of the imagination of faith. Anything less than a cosmic scope risks limiting the scope of Jesus Christ's person and work. Such limitations potentially stunt the formation of the imagination of faith. If faith/trust forms to its object and if our understanding of the person and work of the Son is too small or too narrow, our imagination of faith will be ill-formed, based on a caricature of Christ rather than Christ himself.[4] A couple of key creation texts help shine some light on this point with regard to the cosmic scope of Jesus's person and work: John 1:1–14 and Colossians 1:15–20.

"In the beginning was the Word . . ." (John 1:1 RSV). While perhaps not quite as familiar as John 3:16, the prologue to John's Gospel is among the more well-known texts in Christian Scripture. Reminiscent of Genesis 1:1, the reader is meant to envision the setting of the text as the whole of the cosmos. The eternal Word was with God and was God, *and* all things came into being through him. While there are several varied creation stories within Scripture,[5] for Christians, John 1 is primary among them in that all others are read in relation to it, as through this story, the triune God reveals that place of the eternal Word who became incarnate in Jesus of Nazareth: "And the Word became flesh and lived among us, and we have seen his glory, the glory as of a father's only son, full of grace and truth" (John 1:14). A few crucial points are important to note. First, there is a oneness between the eternal Word and the Father. This thread runs throughout John's Gospel and unfolds how the one incarnate in Jesus Christ reveals the Father by the power of the Spirit (John 14–26). The God of Israel reveals God's self to the world most clearly in the Word incarnate, and it is in, by, and through this very Word that the cosmos came to be. In the Word is life (John 1:4a), and trusting in this Word incarnate, crucified, and risen is life for all who trust in Him (John 3:16, 20). It is this Word that is full of grace and truth, and this truth shall set you free (John 8:31–36). In short, the cosmic Christ *is* the trustworthiness of God made flesh. He does not point to a truth outside of himself.[6] He is the truth incarnate for the sake of the whole cosmos, from its genesis to its completion.

---

4 A cheap example is the WWJD (What would Jesus do?) movement that attempted to use Jesus to explain how kids should use their tingly bits—a reduction of Jesus to a moral standard.

5 Cf. Endo, *Creation and Christology*.

6 See Bonhoeffer's lectures on homiletics at Finkenwalde—e.g., "*The sermon derives from the incarnation of Jesus Christ and is determined by the incarnation of Jesus Christ.* It does not derive from some universal truth or emotional experience. The word of the sermon is the incarnate Christ. The incarnate Christ

This cosmic Christ, the incarnate, crucified, and risen Word, is also personal, as close as the breathing of one's name. Consider Mary Magdalene at the empty tomb shrouded in grief at the death of her friend and Lord (John 20:16–17). Her grief distorted her imagination such that there was a vast chasm between herself and Jesus, so much so that she did not recognize him standing right in front of her. And yet Jesus's whisper of her name cut through the impossibility of the encounter, reconciling her imagination to the reality that the crucified Jesus stood before her risen. Not dead but alive. The cosmic Christ does not mean that Jesus is far off, distant. Rather, it means that the crucified and risen Christ is intimately present with all aspects of the cosmos, we human beings included. We need not recognize the intimacy of the crucified and risen Word for it to be true. When the Word speaks our name, however, the intimacy of this love incarnate is revealed personally—*for you*. The trustworthiness of the triune God encounters us as he encountered Mary. "In the beginning was the Word . . ." Each such moment of trust *is* simultaneously the beginning of creation and time that was once for all *and* the "for you" moment of an unimaginable encounter with One who, though dead, is alive.

The second text is the Christ hymn in the first chapter of Colossians:

> He is the image of the invisible God, the first-born of all creation; for in him all things were created, in heaven and on earth, visible and invisible, whether thrones or dominions or principalities or authorities—all things were created through him and for him. He is before all things, and in him all things hold together. He is the head of the body, the church; he is the beginning, the first-born from the dead, that in everything he might be pre-eminent. For in him all the fulness of God was pleased to dwell, and through him to reconcile to himself all

---

is God. Hence the sermon is actually Christ. God *as* human being. Christ *as* the word. As the Word, Christ walks through the church-community"; Bonhoeffer, *Theological Education at Finkenwalde*, 509–10 (emphasis in the original).

> things, whether on earth or in heaven, making peace by the blood of his cross. (Col 1:15–20 RSV)

In what is akin to a creedal statement perhaps sung by our forebears in faith about the trustworthiness of God in Christ, the text begins and ends with a cosmic vision of who Jesus Christ is and what he has done. With clear resonances to the cosmic scope of John 1, there are three occurrences of *all things* that beg our attention. In Christ, *all things* were created "in heaven and on earth, visible and invisible" (v. 15). In Christ *all things* hold together (v. 17). And through Christ, God reconciles *all things* to God's self through the peacemaking of Christ's cross (v. 20). In terms of the scope of the cosmic Christ, it is important to know a grammatical idiosyncrasy about all things, the Greek τὰ πάντα (*ta PAN-ta*). When this occurs as it does in the Christ hymn (in the neuter plural), there is nothing outside the scope of *all things*. Said another way, grammatically, it does not mean "all things except this one or that one." *All things* means "all things." Hence this text reveals that in Christ, all things were created all over (heaven and earth), that which is perceptible and that which is not: "All things were created through him and for him" (v. 16b). Similarly, in Christ all things hold together. He is the coherence of all things.[7] And ultimately, it is in Christ—in particular, by means of his crucifixion—that God has reconciled all things to God's self. From creation to providence to reconciliation, the scope of Christ's person and work embraces all things. In terms of the person and work of God in Christ, the scope is cosmic. There is nothing beyond or outside of "all things." This is the trustworthiness of God as revealed in Christ Jesus that is cosmic in scope. This is the object of our trust/faith. This is the one in whose image the imagination of faith is formed and in whom the imagination is reconciled. Whether I'm listening to the birds sing from the trees in our backyard or working through a challenging relationship with someone who gets under my skin or

7 The Greek for "hold together" is a form of the verb συνίστημι. In addition to "hold together," this can also carry the nuance of *unite* or *cohere*. Cf. BDAG, ad loc.

doing my best to make sure that all people are welcomed in Jesus's name, these are included in the "all things." This is not an idealism or ideology. This is who God reveals God's self to be in Christ Jesus. This *all things* scope of the good news of the cosmic Christ means that *our* impoverished mercy, fickle love, and self-righteousness should not, do not, and cannot determine the scope of God's love and mercy in Jesus Christ.

The cosmic Christ is before all things. In the cosmic Christ, all things hold together. By way of the crucifixion of the cosmic Christ, all things are reconciled to God. In the incarnation, death, and resurrection of Christ, the triune God reveals God's heart to the world. If the cosmic Christ is the one in whom we trust (have faith), and faith/trust conforms to its object, then the imagination of faith reveals the world, "all things" in Christ Jesus. Paraphrasing Paul, from now on, we regard neither anyone nor anything from a human point of view (2 Cor 5:16). This is the imagination of faith in the cosmic Christ at work, always dependent upon the trustworthiness of trust's object, which is the incarnate, crucified, and risen Word made flesh.

GOD'S COMMITMENT TO THE WORLD REFRACTED THROUGH THE CROSS

As the pinnacle of the Christ hymn in Colossians indicates, it is Christ's death on the cross—specifically, *by the blood of his cross*—that is God's peacemaking with all things. As the telos or completion of the incarnation, Christ's death on the cross is essential to God's self-revelation.[8] God has chosen to reveal and to complete God's ultimate reconciliation of the cosmos to God—God's peacemaking—in and through Jesus's death. Built of paradox, the theology of the cross has God Almighty making God's self small for the world in Jesus Christ. In his sermon "He Who Is the Christ," Paul Tillich illustrates both the content and the form of the theology of the cross. For example,

8 The incarnation of the eternal Word incarnate "is perfected on the cross"; Aulen, *Faith of the Christian Church*, 210.

"One of Luther's most profound insights was that God made [God's self] small for us in Christ. In so doing, [God] left us our freedom and our humanity. [God] showed us [God's] heart, so that our hearts could be won. . . . Those who dream for a better life and try to avoid the Cross as a way, and those who hope for a Christ and attempt to exclude the Crucified, have no knowledge of the mystery of God and of [humanity]."[9] In spite of ourselves, our hopes and dreams for a magic kingdom, suffering and death are unavoidable, whether they be Christ's or our own.[10] We know this because God made God's self small in Jesus Christ so that we creatures might comprehend who God is. God reveals God's very self by concealing it under the broken, crucified body of Jesus hanging on a cross. As such, the content goes hand in glove with the form of paradox. The theology of the cross is built with paradox. What is paradox? It is very much like metaphor in that it is a calculated absurdity. Two opposite things are held together, and meaning is generated from the tension. Take, for example, a quotation attributed to Saint Francis de Sales (1567–1622): "Nothing is so strong as gentleness, nothing as gentle as real strength." And like it, from Paul: "For the [logic] of the cross is folly to those who are perishing, but to us who are being saved it is the power of God" (1 Cor 1:18 RSV). The cross, which is God's foolishness, is at the same time God's saving wisdom. Likewise, God reveals God's self hidden under suffering and death.

Hanging out with Martin Luther for just a wee bit, it was on April 26, 1518—a Friday, for those who are interested—that he released his second album. His first was Ninety-Five Theses on October 31, 1517—a Wednesday. The second was intended to be more low-key. In fact, Luther's superior, Johannes Staupitz, vicar general of the German chapter of the Augustinian Hermits, sent Luther to Heidelberg for a theological get-together, expressly telling him to remain chill. The result of this chill chin-wag in Heidelberg was Luther's most concise outline of a theology of the cross, aptly

9 From Tillich's sermon on Mark 8:27–33; Tillich, "He Who Is the Christ," 148.

10 Another cheap shot, this time at Disneyland.

called his Heidelberg Disputation (1518). Luther's articulation of a theology of the cross remains influential. A glimpse of a few of Luther's theses helps catch the paradoxical nature of the theology of the cross:

> 1. The law of God, the most salutary doctrine of life, cannot advance man on his way to righteousness, but rather hinders him.
> 2. Much less can human works, which are done over and over again with the aid of natural precepts, so to speak, lead to that end.
> 3. Although the works of man always seem attractive and good, they are nevertheless likely to be mortal sins.
> 4. Although the works of God always seem unattractive and appear evil, they are nevertheless really eternal merits.[11]

Key is the upside-down relationship of who God is and what God does and who people are and what people do. God is God. We are not. The fulcrum here is justification. No matter how much we human beings desire to achieve the assurance of salvation through what we do, this effort is working against us. Why? Because it displaces Christ as Lord and Savior. Our human works are seductive in that they appear "attractive and good" (cf. #3). Recall here the noble appearance of our ideologies, whether categorized as conservative or liberal.

Jumping ahead in the disputation, Luther continues,

> 18. It is certain that man must utterly despair of his own ability before he is prepared to receive the grace of Christ.
> 19. That person does not deserve to be called a theologian who looks upon the invisible things of God as though

11 *LW* 31.39.

they were clearly perceptible in those things which have actually happened [Rom 1:20].

20. He deserves to be called a theologian, however, who comprehends the visible and manifest things of God seen through suffering and the cross.
21. A theologian of glory calls evil good and good evil. A theologian of the cross calls the thing what it actually is.[12]

After reinforcing the importance of maintaining the distinction between the proper roles of God and of the human being, with the rhetorical objective being that the human being realizes their dependence upon God for life, Luther turns to the heart of the paradox. God Almighty reveals God's self most clearly hidden under Christ's suffering and death on the cross. The hiddenness of God (*Deus absconditus*) is essential to God being God. God chooses to reveal God's self—God's heart (*Deus revelatis*)—in Christ's suffering and death. This is upside-down. And yet as Luther articulates this paradox of the cross, this is how God has chosen that the world might know who God is: hidden under suffering and the cross.

There are at least three takeaways from the paradox of the cross that help illumine the imagination of faith. The first is the means by which the triune God invites human beings to interpret the work of God: through the cross. Jesus's crucifixion functions interpretively as corrective lenses through which the human vision of the world is refracted in order that we might better see the world as it is in Christ. We will return to this in the next chapter.

The second is that keeping square who God is and who we are is critical to the whole theological enterprise and the imagination of faith. God's movement toward creation with mercy and love is primary. It is the center. When we humans begin to focus on our movement toward God, we can end up taking steps backward. This happens because focusing on what we do is seductive. God has

12 *LW* 31.40.

revealed to the world who God is in Christ's suffering and death *for the sake of the world.* In tow with the incarnation of the Word, God's movement toward the world, toward sinners is one of mercy and love *that cannot be achieved any other way.* Recall that trust/faith forms to its object. The object of trust in Jesus Christ is the Lord and Savior, with his hands stretched out for all the world, for sinners, for you and me. Recall Saint Francis de Sales's teaching: There is nothing so strong as gentleness, nothing so gentle as real strength. Consider Jesus's prayer from the cross: "Father, forgive them, for they do not know what they are doing" (Luke 23:34).

A third takeaway is that the crucified Christ as the triune God's clearest self-revelation is paradoxical. It is absurd. The theology of the cross is rife with paradox, as the cross of Christ *is a paradox.* In, with, and under the suffering and death of the incarnate Word, the God of the whole cosmos reconciles the cosmos to God's self. The glorification of the Word incarnate is the Word's suffering and death.[13] It is about the telos or completion of God's self-emptying (Phil 2:7) as God's victory over sin and death. The upside-down nature of the power dynamics makes the whole thing absurd. God, whose anger can shake the foundations of the mountains, whose mouth can issue a devouring fire, who can swoop down from God's temple on a cherub and fight the enemy, is humiliated and mocked, suffers physical pain and divine abandonment, and dies as a common criminal outside the walls of the holy city.[14] Such is the paradox of the cosmic Christ's peacemaking (Col 1:20).

Like the imaginative nature of a metaphor, the paradox of the cross is an exercise of imagination. It is not reasonable that God, who is all-powerful, would do such a thing. God Almighty, who is more than capable of shaking up a can of divine whoop ass, reveals God's heart to the world hanging on a tree, an abomination. This act of God, accessible via the imagination of faith, defies the logic and

13 The Johannine theme of Christ's crucifixion—his being lifted up on the cross—as his glorification, an image built on Moses lifting up the serpent in the wilderness; cf. John 3 and Num 21.

14 Images of the God of Israel as Divine Warrior—e.g., 2 Sam 22 and Ps 18.

reason of our created world: "Has not God made foolish the wisdom of the world?" (1 Cor 1:20). What we humans are left with is God's unconditional commitment to the cosmos and God's reconciliation of the cosmos through Christ's death and his blood shed on the cross. This paradox is revealed in faith through trusting in Jesus Christ. As Douglas John Hall puts it, "Faith's assumption that the cross of Christ marks, in a decisive and irrevocable way, the unconditional participation of God in the life of the world, the concretization of God's love for the world, the commitment of God to the fulfillment of creation's promise. 'God so loved the world that he gave his only son . . .' (John 3:16)."[15]

The cross of Christ *is* the trustworthiness of God. This is God revealing who God is and what God does. The cross is the trustworthiness that invites our trust and our entrusting the whole of our life and the whole of the cosmos to the triune God, who is love. Like how light through a prism reveals a full spectrum of color, so in faith the world is revealed as refracted through the cross of Christ.

Such is the foolishness of God—that is, God's wisdom—that reveals the heart of God, the trustworthiness of God, to the world via Christ's incarnation, which is completed on the cross. This is the fullness of God's commitment to what and who God has created. Even more so, in the fullness of Jesus Christ, the eternal, incarnate Word, "Jesus reveals what divinity is." Ian McFarland continues (it's a long quote, but hang in there; it's important),

> For in that Jesus is God the Word made flesh, the whole of his life from birth through death and resurrection reveals that God, the Creator of all things visible and invisible, eternal and transcendent, who alone "has immortality and dwells in unapproachable light" (1 Tim. 6:16), refuses to be God apart from human beings—indeed, refuses to be God except as a human being. Although human beings in their sin would seek to live apart from God, thereby securing for themselves

15 Hall, *Cross in Our Context*, 35.

> only the utter and irrevocable certainty of death (Rom. 6:23), God renders this impossible by the Word (who is God) taking on "the likeness of sinful flesh" (8:3), thereby demonstrating that God is God in just this way and no other. So it is that the entirety of Jesus' life is his "work," for it is in all that he does, and indeed, just as he does all that he does (that is, in and through the concrete activities of hungering, thirsting, tiring, tasting, smelling, eating, drinking, sleeping, standing, walking, sweating, speaking, hearing, rejoicing, fearing, suffering, and dying), that he is Jesus and, as Jesus, God as well.[16]

McFarland's focus on the fleshiness of Jesus's incarnation brings the cosmic, crucified Christ—the one in whom the Christian trusts—into clear view. The mystery of the cosmic and the paradox of the cross are only made more fulsome by drawing also into view "all that [Jesus] does." In this, the triune God grants the world a glimpse of God, whose commitment to the cosmos and all its constituent parts, including you and me, is complete.

DEATH, RESURRECTION, AND WONDER

Olaf Roy Wicker was a friend of my grandfather with whom I spent a good deal of time as a child. His flowing gray locks made him appear ancient long before he actually was.[17] He was blessed with a dry, sardonic sense of humor. With this and an overall crusty demeanor, he walked into the bank in the small Minnesota town where he lived one morning in the late 1980s. The young, chipper teller at the window greeted him warmly, as I am sure she was instructed to do: "Good morning, Mr. Wicker! How are you today?" Olaf Roy responded dryly, "I'm slowly dying."

16 McFarland, *Word Made Flesh*, 219–20.

17 Olaf Roy Wicker, 1916–2017.

You and I, all of our family and friends, our neighbors and enemies . . . we will all die. So will the cosmos and all that is in it.[18] Despite our mighty efforts to avoid this reality, we all live within the horizon of death.[19] Olaf Roy, even though he was being a bit of an ass for his own giggles, was correct. Even at our most vigorous, our horizon is entropy. We share this quality with grass and trees, our parents and our children, our neighbors and our enemies, and the cosmos as a whole. Death is perhaps the universal common denominator, and its denial is a root challenge for the imagination of faith, for without death, there can be no resurrection.

Trusting in Jesus is about death and life, especially insofar as the object of this trust, the eternal, incarnate Word, Jesus Christ, died and was raised from the dead. Christ's incarnation, death, and resurrection are the trustworthiness of God that undergirds the imagination of faith. Christ's resurrection is the turn that puts the whole death-to-life promise into perspective.

To get at this, abide for a moment in 1 Corinthians 15, wherein Paul makes clear that the resurrection is pivotal to faith and to the world that trusting in Jesus Christ reveals. He begins with this critical tale:

> For I delivered to you as of first importance what I also received, that Christ died for our sins in accordance with the scriptures, that he was buried, that he was raised on the third day in accordance with the scriptures, and that he appeared to Cephas, then to the twelve. Then he appeared to more than five hundred [folks] at one time, most of whom are still alive, though some have fallen asleep. Then he appeared to James, then to all the apostles. Last of all, as to one untimely born, he appeared also to me. For I am the least of the apostles, unfit to

18 Here I have in mind entropy and the second law of thermodynamics. For (something close to) a nonspecialist introduction to the second law of thermodynamics, cf. Ben-Naim, *Entropy Demystified*.

19 Cf. Becker, *Denial of Death*.

> be called an apostle, because I persecuted the church of God. (1 Cor 15:3–9 RSV)

While it chafes me that Paul excludes the women, especially Mary Magdalene, he appeals to the witness of those who experienced the crucified and risen Jesus. Jesus died. Jesus was raised from the dead. Trustworthy people saw him, as unbelievable and unimaginable as it was. Unlike Lazarus and others that Jesus returned to life and eventually died again, Jesus's resurrection was a different thing.[20] His resurrection was not putting off death for another day. Christ's death was the defeat of death's power. As such, it was a contravention of the experienced order of the universe. This is not how things are supposed to roll. If the horizon of the whole of the cosmos is entropy, decay, and death, this business about the crucified (i.e., really and fully dead!) and risen Christ is an anomaly. But it's a critical anomaly. Like the cosmic Christ, the death and resurrection of Jesus are essential for the animation of the imagination of faith.

Trusting in Jesus's fullness—eternal, incarnate, crucified, *and risen* Word—is what this Christian existence is about. According to Paul, "If there is no resurrection of the dead, then Christ has not been raised; if Christ has not been raised, then our preaching is in vain and your faith is in vain" (1 Cor 15:13–14 RSV). Who Jesus is (i.e., eternal Word incarnate) and what Jesus did (i.e., died and rose) *are* the heart of the triune God's trustworthiness for the individual and for the whole of the cosmos. And this is the window into

---

20 With Lazarus, it is clear that he was raised to life to die another day; cf. John 11. This is also the case for other such resuscitations, whether by prophets (1 Kgs 17:17–24; 2 Kgs 4:18–37; 13:20–21), Jesus (Luke 7:11–17; 8:49–56), Peter (Acts 9:36–42), or Paul (20:7–12). Presumably, this list should also include those who were raised in the immediate wake of Jesus's death (Matt 27:23–23). A footnote to the footnote, this last vignette, not mentioned by Paul himself, is perhaps one of the funniest tales in Christian Scripture. While Paul was preaching—seemingly banging on and on—the young chap Eutychus was sitting on a windowsill, fell asleep, and fell out of the window to his death. How many times have we who preached killed poor Eutychus?

wonder. What could be more delightfully and strangely wonderful than Christ overcoming the power of death?

We live our lives within the horizon of death. Dear Olaf Roy's words to the bank teller were true. We are slowly dying. Neither Ponce de Leone's sixteenth-century quest for the fountain of youth nor contemporary cryogenics, for all their effort, can reverse the inevitability of decay and death. Worm food we all shall be. Entropy is inevitable.

Recalling the trust algebra from the previous chapter (X → Y for Z), the Lord God does not promise that trusting in Jesus will exempt anyone from death. A person trusts Jesus for healing, for wholeness, for forgiveness, for life (John 8:51). Death is a common denominator. One can ponder Enoch and Elijah as exceptions to the rule.[21] One can also ponder Jesus's words: "Very truly, I tell you, whoever keeps my word will never see death" (John 8:51). It could well be that no one has kept Jesus's word, given that everyone since has met the same end with the worms. Trusting in Jesus Christ, Paul's words serve as a guide: "For the love of Christ controls us, because we are convinced that one has died for all; therefore all have died" (2 Cor 5:14 RSV).[22] In Christ, all have died. And therefore, "If we have died with Christ, we believe that we shall also live with him. For we know that Christ being raised from the dead will never die again; death no longer has dominion over him. The death he died he died to sin, once for all, but the life he lives he lives to God. So you also must consider yourselves dead to sin and alive to God in Christ Jesus" (Rom 6:8–11 RSV). I realize that this does not make the experience or reality of death any easier. Save for Enoch and Elijah, all experience death. Trusting in Jesus does not change the truth of Olaf Roy's comment. Indeed, we are all slowly dying. Yet Christ's death changes the nature of our death because of the wonderful promise of the resurrection that in

21 Neither Enoch (Gen 5:24) nor Elijah (2 Kgs 2:11–12) experienced death, but both were taken into the presence of God. Interestingly, both have been the subject of intense speculation over the centuries.

22 My gratitude goes to Jennifer Agee for her assistance with this insight.

faith spills over upon the world. Death's sting remains, but Christ has taken away death's power.[23]

All of this is rather highfalutin theological speak. There is a reason that, for centuries, Christians have been drawn to the butterfly and to the seed, both of which are everyday approximations of death making way for life. Within the caterpillar's sarcophagus-like cocoon, there is transformation and a birth into a new life.[24] A seed falls into the earth and dies (John 12:24), only to yield the sprout that breaks through the cold earth in search of the sun. The resurrection is so unbelievably and unimaginably wild that we benefit from images that open our imagination to the promise that we not only live within the horizon of death.

We can live within a narrative where the caterpillar enters the cocoon and that's it, or where the seed falls into the earth and kaput, or where death is the final word. Many of us do. Pew sitters, deacons—pastors, even. There is a constant tension between the narrative of death and the narrative of life, each of which has the capacity to capture the imagination, to hold it, to guide it, to form it.

THE OBJECT OF TRUST AND EUCATASTROPHE

The Christian lives in a state of tension between two narratives, one of death and one of life. The imagination of faith, conformed to its object of trust—that is, the eternal Word incarnate, crucified and risen—reveals the narrative of life, wherein the sinner (again, all of us, see Rom 3:23) is defined by who Jesus is and what Jesus did rather than by what they have done. We are defined by Christ's death, wherein our death has been transformed by Christ, emptying it of its

23 Note the dynamic of the burial of Stephen, deacon and martyr: "Devout men buried Stephen, and made great lamentation over him" (Acts 8:2 RSV). They are devout, meaning that they trust in the power of Jesus's resurrection, and they still grieve. The two are not mutually exclusive.

24 Have a listen to Dan Reeder's "Born a Worm," MP3 audio, track 10 on Dan Reeder, *Every Which Way*, Oh Boy Records, 2020, as a contemporary introit for Easter.

power. Trusting in Jesus, the Christian is freed from the power of sin and death and invited to imagine (the imagination of faith) that this is true of the whole world. All things means all things (Col 1:15–20). Such a vision *in faith in Jesus Christ* remains in tension with lived experience. Old creation and new creation in a kind of competition.

In 1938, J. R. R. Tolkien delivered a lecture, "On Fairy Stories," at the University of St. Andrews. In this lecture about the art of the fairy story, Tolkien explored the realm of Faërie, the world that serves as the setting for the fairy story. In his words, limiting fairy stories to "stories about fairies" is "too narrow." Rather, "It is too narrow, even if we reject the diminutive size, for fairy-stories are not in normal English usage stories *about* fairies or elves, but stories about Fairy, that is *Faërie*, the realm or state in which fairies have their being. *Faërie* contains many things besides elves and fays, and besides dwarfs, witches, trolls, giants, or dragons: it holds the seas, the sun, the moon, the sky; and the earth, and all things that are in it: tree and bird, water and stone, wine and bread, and ourselves, mortal men, when we are enchanted."[25] Tolkien describes competing narratives. The world is the same in both. What is different is whether the person is enchanted or not. In other words, there are multiple layers of reality, and those who are enchanted—that is, those who have given themselves in full to the fullness of Faërie—are able to see reality *as it is*. Being *in Faërie* helps the reader not only see what others don't but see what everyone does see anew.

To be clear, to speak of Faërie is not equivalent to speaking of the gospel. There is, however, a critical analogy. The world that the imagination of faith reveals functions similarly to Faërie as described by Tolkien. Trusting in Jesus opens the world as not only old creation, as not only the world lived within the horizon of death. Trusting in Jesus reveals a world reconciled to God in Christ—all things. Tolkien speaks of the power of fairy stories to recover wonder at the world around us, the world that is visible: "Recovery (which includes return and renewal of health) is a re-gaining—regaining a clear view. I do

25 Tolkien, "On Fairy Stories," 9.

not say 'seeing things as they are' and involve myself with the philosophers, though I might venture to say 'seeing things as we are (or were) meant to see them'—as things apart from ourselves. We need, in any case, to clean our windows; so that the things seen clearly may be freed from our drab blur of triteness or familiarity—from possessiveness."[26] With not a little bit of trembling, I'll push Tolkien's observation here to say the gospel, the narrative of God's trustworthiness, does indeed invite us to see things *as they are in Christ*. The imagination of faith does clean our windows, freeing us from only seeing the world as it appears to be, from living life within the horizon of death, in order to see the world as it is in Jesus Christ, whose death has reconciled all things.

Tolkien identifies an essential element of the fairy story as the "eucatastrophe." He is playing with the word *catastrophe*, with its Greek roots lineage, κατά (*ka-TA*, against) and στρωφεῖν (*stro-PHANE*, to turn), but he adds the prefix εὖ (often pronounced *you* or *hĕ-oo*), which means "good." The catastrophe is, as many of us use it, an occurrence that turns out to be a shitmess. The *eucatastrophe* is the opposite of a turn into a shitmess. Tolkien calls the "happy ending" a "sudden joyous 'turn' (for there is no end to any fairy-tale)."[27] The story of Faërie does not end, but the eucatastrophe *is* a joyous turn that serves as the ultimate (but not the only) point of the whole. Tolkien himself makes the observation that the gospel is like this, saying, "The Birth of Christ is the eucatastrophe of Man's history. The Resurrection is the eucatastrophe of the story of the incarnation."[28]

The truth that Tolkien's analysis of the art of the fairy story reveals shares the dynamics of the freedom that accompanies the imagination of faith. That is the freedom in envisioning the world as it has been reconciled in Christ. The truth of such a world is not a thin

26 Tolkien, 58.

27 Tolkien, 68.

28 Tolkien, 72. He says further that the art of the fairy story "has been verified. God is Lord, of angels, and of men—and of elves. Legend and History have met and fused" (73).

veneer but a deep truth that begins with "we are all sinners"[29] and ends with Christ becoming the greatest sinner of all for the sake of the world. That is, Christ takes on *all the sins of the world.*[30] This reveals the world as it is reconciled in Christ, a world accessible via the imagination of faith.

PERPETUAL TENSION BETWEEN OLD CREATION AND NEW CREATION

The reconciliation of the imagination in Christ is not a one-and-done reality. Truth be told, the Christian lives in an awkward dance between the failed and the reconciled imagination. There are pressures upon the imagination of faith, perhaps first among them being experience. No matter our intentions, we humans experience ourselves and others outside of Christ. How often do we find ourselves judging another person or ourselves as if Christ's death for sinners were not true?

Experience is often wrought with tension between reality and reality, between old creation and new. The first reality is the old creation, which we fully inhabit, wherein we define ourselves and others by our failings and failures, by our sin. Where we look at the other, whether the "other" is another human or at ourselves in the mirror, only to see that someone trusting in that which is not God. Where we see only bad faith manifesting itself in its many guises. I have met very few people, including myself, who are not quick to judge. This bad-faith judgment squirts out sideways, sounding like fear or hate, snootiness or

29 "Now join with us prodigious and hardened sinners lest you diminish Christ for us. . . . You can be a bogus sinner and have Christ for a fictitious savior. Instead, get used to the fact that Christ is a genuine savior and that you are a real sinner"; Luther to Spalatin, August 21, 1544, quoted in Hendrix, *Martin Luther*, 270; WABr 10.639.

30 Luther on Gal 3:13: Christ "has and bears all the sins of all men in His body—not in the sense that He has committed them but in the sense that He took these sins, committed by us, upon His own body, in order to make satisfaction for them with His own blood"; *LW* 26.277.

envy. Theologically, such judgment is always a declaration, spoken or not, of the unrighteousness of the other.

So are our judgments necessarily incorrect? Is there no unrighteousness in ourselves, in our neighbor, or in our enemy? Is there no bad faith? Clearly, there is. We needn't look any further than our bathroom mirror. People do stupid and destructive things. Human history can be written as a series of examples of human folly and wickedness wherein jealousy, hate, and fear have laid claim to the imagination. In a world created by such an imagination, our eyes and hearts are covered with cataracts that obscure the world as it is in Christ, the new creation in Christ.

Peter Maurin (1877–1949), cofounder of the Catholic Worker Movement with Dorothy Day (1897–1980), was known to speak of the "art of human contacts." In her autobiography, Day describes Maurin's disposition: "It was seeing Christ in others, loving the Christ you saw in others. Greater than this, it was having faith in the Christ in others without being able to see Him. Blessed is he that believes without seeing."[31] The Catholic Worker Movement was born of the Great Depression, a perfect storm of economic, environmental, and social collapse that resulted in poverty, displacement, and despair for millions. This is to say, the people who Day and Maurin were walking with daily were in a bad state—sick, demoralized, addicted, ragged, despairing, down and out. The Catholic Worker Movement worked to feed and shelter these folks and to assist them in rediscovering their dignity. They still do. At the foundation of this movement was this simple and small window into the new creation as seen through faith, through a reconciled imagination.[32] Blessed is the one who trusts without seeing. This art of human contact, as Maurin called it, exemplifies living with both realities held in tension. It is not utopian but realistic. The new creation breaking into the old, putting the old creation in proper perspective.

---

31 Day, *Long Loneliness*, 171.

32 Luther: "Faith is a constant gaze that looks at nothing except Christ, the Victor over sin and death and the Dispenser of righteousness, salvation, and eternal life"; *LW* 26.356.

The imagination reconciled in faith in Jesus Christ is not utopian. It is realistic in that it accepts that human life and the life of the cosmos exist within the horizon of death and within the life of Christ. As such, there is suffering and sorrow, sin and death, *and* joy and wonder, resurrection and life. The crucifixion of the eternal, incarnate Word holds these two realities together. In full solidarity with creation, including creation's suffering and death, the incarnation of the Word echoes God's pronouncement of creation as "very good" (Gen 1:31) while taking the fullness of that creation, including sin and death, into God's self, holding reality and reality together, reconciling the old into the new in the fullness of time.

When we look into the mirror, then, we see both realities. Being a Christian means trusting in Christ Jesus. It means faith. Trusting in Jesus does not erase suffering, sorrow, sin, and death. Trusting in Jesus reconciles the imagination to see the world in and through Jesus Christ. Blessed is the one who believes without seeing.

TRUSTING IN JESUS IS PROPER FREEDOM

Luther's "Freedom of a Christian" (1520) presents a particular challenge. Within the popular discourse of the United States, freedom can have a libertarian texture, à la Patrick Henry's "Give Me Liberty or Give Me Death!" speech.[33] Such patriotic verve! And yet for whom is this liberty? Certainly not those brought by force from Africa to the plantations of the American South. Certainly not the women who would wait nearly another 150 years for the right to vote. The common air that we breathe in the United States has been charged from before the birth of the nation with freedom, but not freedom of all. So how does one help students think critically about the thin popularist notion of freedom and from there consider something more substantive like freedom in Luther's treatise on Christian liberty?

33 Patrick Henry, "Give Me Liberty or Give Me Death!," speech to the Virginia Convention, March 23, 1775.

Luther speaks of Christian liberty and faith as synonyms. The Christian's freedom is dependent upon their trust in Jesus Christ above all else, no matter what "all else" may be: "This is that Christian liberty, our faith, which does not induce us to live in idleness or wickedness but makes the law and works unnecessary for any man's righteousness and salvation."[34] Through trusting in Jesus, what belongs to Jesus becomes the believer's. Hence as noted earlier, Christ takes on the sin of the world and in exchange grants us his righteousness. Salvation—that is, being freed from the power of sin and death—frees the individual to live *not for themselves* but for the other, for the neighbor. There are two "propositions" that Luther uses as scaffolding for the argument:

> A Christian is a perfectly free lord of all, subject to none.
> A Christian is a perfectly dutiful servant of all, subject to all.[35]

The first thesis is of concern here; the second will return as a concern in the final chapter of this book.[36]

The texture of freedom, as Luther describes it, is commensurate with what has already been explored in his articulation of the theology of the cross in the Heidelberg Disputation. Freedom in Christ is a result of faith alone. This freedom is God's work, as it begins with the human being's trust in God's trustworthiness—the incarnate, crucified, and risen Word made flesh. God in Christ justifies—makes right—the sinner through trust/faith. In this treatise, like three legs of a stool, Luther identifies three powers of trusting in Jesus Christ: (1) freedom from the power of sin and death, (2) recognizing God as God, and (3) the unification of the believer

---

34 Martin Luther, "Freedom of a Christian," in *LW* 31.349–50.

35 *LW* 31.344.

36 When one moves too quickly to Luther's second thesis, foregoing the necessary formation that accompanies the first, the result is ideology posing as Christianity, ethics with little interest in Christ but for him as an example.

with Christ.[37] Existential and eschatological freedom come with trusting in Jesus. The imagination of faith is a confluence of these three points. In trusting in Jesus, one is freed from the power of sin and death; one is reminded of one's creatureliness and God's Godness, and one is unified with Christ himself. This is the point of Christianity. This is freedom in faith.

CONCLUSION

If we are indeed living in an age of bad faith, then consider the three legs of the "bad faith" stool: (1) bad faith has one enslaved to the power of sin and death; (2) bad faith mistakes imitation golden calves, whether they be things, relationships, power, or ideology for God; and (3) bad faith projects a world in which the individual is alienated from Christ, a world wherein something else is as Christ is Lord and Savior. In such a "place," the imagination is captive to death and formed toward that which cannot ultimately give life.

By way of the eucatastrophe that is the incarnation, death, and resurrection of the cosmic Christ, the triune God reveals God's heart to the world and reveals the world to itself as a world redeemed in Jesus Christ, a world visible at least in part (1 Cor 13:12) via the imagination of faith.[38] Borrowing the psalmist's words, the imagination of faith envisions the kiss of Psalm 85 as the eucatastrophe, where God turns the world one heart at a time toward life:

---

37 *LW* 31.347–53.

38 "In both these contexts, it is easy to agree with Tolkien that it matters less where fairy stories came from, or what they might originally have referred to, than what they have to give the reader in that now which he so strongly emphasized. For just as there will always be war, so, in Tolkien's view, there will always be fairy stories, even if he has to write them himself. If we have the one, we surely need the other. We need fairy stories to give us those very things that he listed so carefully—recovery of a more hopeful reality, escape from the imminent shadow of death, and consolation for sorrow through the eucatastrophe that turns catastrophe to joy"; Flieger, *There Would Always*, 15–16.

> Steadfast love and faithfulness will meet;
> righteousness and peace will kiss each other.
> (Ps 85:10 RSV)

In this kiss, the world—*all things*—is revealed in Christ as the world reconciled to God. Such a vision accompanies trusting in Jesus Christ. While our capacity to envision reality in Christ is always partial, when it comes into focus, it is a beautiful thing. The powers of sin and death, fear and hate, melt away as the crucified and risen Christ shows up behind the locked doors of our hearts, saying, "Peace be with you."[39]

39 Riffing here off Kierkegaard, who wrote in his journal sometime in April 1838 regarding the crucified and risen Christ's appearances to his disciples behind locked doors (John 20): "If [Christ] is to come and dwell in me, it will have to happen in accordance with the almanac heading containing the gospel verse for the day: [Christ] enters through closed doors"; Kierkegaard, *Kierkegaard's Journals and Notebooks*, 2:92.

CHAPTER FIVE

The World Refracted

> There is another world, but it is this one.
>
> —Paul Éluard

> Imagination. Could there be any concept more vague, more overused, more slippery, and more subject to the whims and idiosyncrasies of its countless users?
>
> —Garrett Green, *Imagining Theology*

When light passes through a prism, it exits broken into its fullness, at least a fuller fullness available to the human eye. From that which has no color, the refraction opens up the light to reveal a rainbow of color. Roy G. Biv, as I recall. The prism does not make the color; the color spectrum is already there. The prism reveals it.

"There is another world, and it is this one."[1] The imagination of faith does not transport the person into another world. It opens our vision of this world to see it as it is reconciled in Christ. In Christ's incarnation, death, and resurrection, reconciliation has happened, both cosmically and individually. Our imaginations are perpetually captive to the gravitational pull of sin and death. The reconciliation of

---

1 Words often attributed to French poet Paul Éluard. Cited by Hollis, *Archetypal Imagination*, 4. Cf. McKenzie Wark's exploration of the slippery origin of the saying in his blog post "There Is Another World, and It Is This One," Public Seminar, January 14, 2014, accessed July 31, 2022, https://publicseminar.org/2014/01/there-is-another-world-and-it-is-this-one/.

the imagination, which happens through faith/trust in Jesus Christ, frees the person to see the world as it is, ultimately captive to the gravitational pull of life in Christ. The imagination of faith frees us to see the world in full color as it is refracted in and through Jesus Christ. There is another world, and it is this one.

There is freedom in trusting in Jesus Christ, and this freedom is the imagination of faith. The imagination of faith cannot and should not be reduced to a method. Neither the scientific method nor any other method will move the imagination of faith forward. The imagination of faith is a disposition toward the whole of life *as if the cosmos has been reconciled in the incarnation, death, and resurrection of Jesus Christ.* To be clear, the imagination of faith is not a synonym for a cheery disposition. Trusting in Jesus does not transform the world into a syrupy mess of puppies and unicorns. The imagination of faith does not make the whole world into a thin Disney facade, a new even magicier kingdom. The world refracted in faith in the Crucified One frees one to see the world as it is and as it is in Christ, who experienced real suffering, abandonment, and death. The same world is reconciled in Christ—defined by his death and life, not by our entropy and death alone.

This chapter explores the imagination of faith in Jesus Christ as a disposition that informs reading Scripture, preaching, and living in this world. A particular pickle with the use of imagination is that it can be difficult to pin down, perhaps not being as epistemologically rigorous as many would like. To this, I say: that's accurate. Garrett Green's question is not off the mark: Could there be any concept more vague, more overused, more slippery, and more subject to the whims and idiosyncrasies of its countless users?[2] Like Green, I am convinced that while potentially slippery, engaging people's imaginations is

---

2 Green's work in *Imagining Theology* is an excellent read, differently (i.e., more systematically) rigorous than this little tome. Green leaves his readers with a charge of sorts, two tasks for Christianity in a post-Christian age. The first of these is that Christian theology must "take leave of the imagination-versus-reality way of thinking once and for all" (263), and the second task "is to give up the quest for certainty . . . to stop looking for certainty in the wrong places" (266).

the way forward in a post-Christian age. Hope beyond the current dry rot is in the transformative power of faith, of trusting in Jesus. Framing this with imagination, a superpower common to all humans (yes, nerds, this means imagination is just a regular power), invites people into a cruciform vision of the world.

ON INTERPRETATION

Reading and thus interpreting are central movements to Christianity given that Christianity is a scriptural religion. Christian Scripture is the primary locus wherein the triune God reveals God's self to the world. There is something about being on a journey that serves as a metaphor for interpreting Scripture. Along the way, often in a mix of confusion and curiosity, the horizons of Scripture unfold and illuminate the world. Oftentimes this illumination is of a tiny corner of the cosmos; sometimes it is the whole of the cosmos illuminated.

CHRIST ALONG THE WAY

The road to Emmaus (Luke 24:13–35) is one such journey where the imagination of faith was kindled to illuminate the cosmos. At the start of the journey, the world as Cleopas and the other disciple knew it was shrouded by grief and confusion. Hopes were dashed. Death and its forces had won. Jesus was dead. Whatever hopes that they had for change or fulfillment, for the redemption of Israel (Luke 24:21), died with him. So when a stranger begins walking with them and he appears clueless about the catastrophe that now enveloped them, it makes sense that their "eyes were kept from recognizing him" (Luke 24:16). Though *the crucified and risen Christ was right there in front of them speaking with them*, they could not see him. Why? He was dead. Death is death is death. The world that we create by way of our imagination has been formed to interpret death as death, and when you're dead, you're dead. Why would their imaginations predict anything else?

What transpires along the road to Emmaus has a good bit to say about the imagination of faith. The story is ultimately about being encountered by the risen Lord. The shape of the encounter is that of Christian worship. Jesus accompanies the folks on the road, encountering them in the fabric of their reality, which in this instance is grief and confusion. Even though they had heard an unimaginable tale from Mary Magdalene, Joanna, and Mary the mother of James—a tale that Jesus's tomb was empty but for angels that told them that Jesus was alive—they were enveloped by the unfolding of death. After hearing their account of things, the stranger chides them a wee bit. Why? To paraphrase, *O foolish folks, why are you so slow of heart to trust all that the prophets said?* (Luke 24:25–26). Their fault here was not their grief or confusion. It was their inability to trust in the promise of who Jesus was and what Jesus did. The stranger does not abandon them. Rather, Jesus, right there with them but still hidden from their eyes, interprets the Scripture to them in light of himself. As Luke says, "And beginning with Moses and all the prophets, he interpreted to them in all the scriptures the things concerning himself" (Luke 24:27 RSV). This is key to the imagination of faith with regard to interpretation. The risen Lord, still a stranger, remains with, accompanies, reveals, and stokes the imagination of faith with regard to the Scriptures. Their eyes still did not fully see, so clouded were their imaginations to the possibility that death itself had been defeated. And yet they recalled later that their hearts were moved while the "stranger" taught them along the way. This reflection comes at the table upon arriving in Emmaus. Out of hospitality, the disciples invite their companion in for shelter and nourishment. The tables are turned, however, when the stranger is revealed in the breaking of bread. The stranger, now a guest, becomes the host. Jesus is not the one transformed in this encounter. The transformation is of the disciples' vision. Their imagination of death is transformed into an imagination of faith in Jesus Christ. Reading and interpreting Scripture is about being encountered by the crucified and risen Christ along the way.

Christian reading, then, is not about conquering the text. Instead, Christ the stranger meets us wherever we are strolling, accompanied by our imagination of death, and transforms our imagination into the imagination of faith in Christ Jesus, the risen one who has transformed death into life. This encounter, of which the weekly gathering of the Christian community around Word and Sacrament is an analog, is the continual transformation toward trust, ultimately confirmed by our hands opened and outstretched to receive Him who is our life, to receive the tangible trustworthiness of God incarnate. While we might have other ends in interpreting Christian Scripture, they are all at best penultimate to being encountered by the living Word.

Interpreting Christian Scripture is not ultimately about employing the proper method. Instead, trust is the primary disposition of the Christian reader of the Bible. The imagination of faith, which sees everything in and through the crucified and risen Christ, is primary. From the vantage point of trust in Jesus, the reader can employ a whole host of methods in service of this end. The disposition of trust illuminates the text toward faith and life in Jesus's name.

TO WHOM DOES SCRIPTURE WITNESS?

An important question to consider along the way is, *To whom does Scripture witness?*

There is a lot hanging on how this question is answered. Let's say that there are three basic answers: the triune God, human beings, or both, with priority given to the triune God. Lest this be a mystery novel, let me be clear that I am convinced that the third option is what is needed today. While Scripture bears any number of metaphorical human fingerprints, the Bible witnesses to the triune God. Said differently, the triune God reveals God's self to the world by way of this amazingly messy book, with a variegated history of interpretation and some tattered edges. Scripture does not have the character of a to-the-point memo from the boss, complete with a bulleted list of action items. Scripture is far more interesting and illusive as it bears witness to its Main Character against the backdrop of an array of complex worlds.

Now that my cards are on the table, return to the question: *To whom does Scripture witness?* Historic answers to this question reveal in very broad strokes the history of the Bible's interpretation and perhaps a glimpse of its future. At the risk of a vast oversimplification of the history of biblical interpretation, here it goes.[3]

Somewhere between the early seventeenth century and the mid-nineteenth century, a slow shift began in how biblical interpreters answered the question.[4] Prior to the shift, if you asked the interpreter to whom the biblical text witnesses, their first answer in one way or another would be the triune God. After the shift, the interpreter would give priority to humans. Interpretation prior to the shift is considered "precritical" and after "critical,"[5] the language revealing an obvious prejudice toward the critical. As this shift solidified and acquired its own doctrinaire quality,[6] biblical scholars moved from focusing first on what this text reveals about who the triune God is to focusing on what the text says about who people were and are.[7] From a theological/revelatory focus to an anthropological one.

---

3 This oversimplification will make specialists cringe. More robust treatments of the history of biblical interpretation are available. For a collection of excerpts from interpreters throughout the history of the church, see Yarchin, *History of Biblical Interpretation.* For more summative looks at major movements within the history of biblical interpretation, both Christian and Jewish, see the three volumes edited by Hauser and Watson, *History of Biblical Interpretation.* For a look at the progression with regard to a particular biblical book, see Childs, *Struggle to Understand.*

4 Whether with Descartes (1596–1650), Spinoza (1632–77) in the seventeenth century, or the likes of Benjamin Jowett (1817–93) in the nineteenth, we live and interpret in the wake of the shift.

5 For a seminal exploration of this interpretive shift, cf. Steinmetz, "Superiority of Pre-critical Exegesis."

6 Recall the discussion in chapter 1 of Childs's diagnosis of dry rot with the 1979 publication of his *Introduction to the Old Testament.*

7 As with Newton's second law of motion, the momentum of scholarship moves from the scholar to the student and, since many of these students are clergy, from clergy to congregant. If biblical scholarship has little interest in

In the words of Michael Legaspi, "Scripture died a quiet death in Western Christendom some time in the sixteenth century," and in its place came "biblical studies." That is, the study of the Bible moved from an exercise of faith to an academic exercise in a postconfessional framework.[8] In other words, creedal commitments (recall that *creed* comes from *credo*, "I trust") were no longer seen as legitimate lenses through which to best interpret the Bible. This movement in the study of the Bible meant that the sociohistorical took center stage, as this approach could cut through the layers of churchy frosting imposed upon an otherwise pristine layer cake—layers of the history of and behind the biblical text. The starting assumption that Scripture witnessed to God during the precritical shifted to an assumption that the Bible witnessed to sociocultural, anthropological fingerprints—reading Scripture to see what it says about us and our forebears rather than reading Scripture for what it reveals about God.

This shift from the precritical to the critical, while far more complex and less clean than the previous description, is thoroughly instantiated at present, so much so that professional biblical interpreters (e.g., clergy) can complete their studies without focusing on the theological question. That said, there are significant gains that have come with the shift, but there are also aspects that we have forgotten.

In terms of gains, biblical interpreters and the Bible itself have been unleashed from certain unhealthy and unbiblical ecclesial controls. Historical, literary, and cultural knowledge of the worlds behind and reflected by the text have been explored, our knowledge broadened, and critiques offered. Biblical interpreters have come to understand some significantly lopsided aspects of Scripture, not least of which is the relative absence of female characters and voices within largely patriarchal religious and cultural systems. These gains provide additional texture to the biblical witness.

---

the text's witness to the triune God, eventually the minister attempting to interpret the text will share this little interest. Such is the extent of the dry rot.

8 Legaspi, *Death of Scripture*. Also cf. Frei, *Eclipse of Biblical Narrative*; and Rae, *History and Hermeneutics*.

What has been forgotten? One major thing. We have forgotten the theological framework within which the Bible is understandable as Christian Scripture. In the interest of untethering the Bible from (sometimes real, sometimes perceived) ecclesial mishandling, the rule of faith has been the proverbial baby thrown out with the bathwater. *To whom does Scripture witness?* In the absence of the triune God, we are left with a Bible that we look to for what it says about human beings, culture, history, and so on. We have lost the imagination of faith as a disposition for reading and interpreting Scripture. When we search Scripture, seeking reflections of ourselves, that is what we will find.

To wrap up this detour from the task at hand, what I (and others) suggest is that we move toward a postcritical engagement with Scripture.[9] It is both impossible and unhelpful to attempt to divorce the reading of the Bible from a sociohistorically conditioned consciousness that has been gained in recent times. In terms of knowledge, we have gained a great deal about the origins and content of biblical texts—the Bible's varied textures. Our understanding of biblical texts, their sociocultural contexts, and biblical interpretation is enriched by methods of exploration that expose patriarchal, misogynistic, and colonial aspects of the text itself as well as centuries of often-harmful

---

9 *Postcritical* is a term already in use, probably originating with Lindbeck, *Nature of Doctrine*, 122f. While I do not always agree with the theological use of those who employ the approach, I find the term's theological and historically descriptive quality useful. Here is a summary of the basic postcritical interpretive assumption: "'Postcritical Scriptural Interpretation' refers to an emergent tendency among Jewish and Christian scholars and theologians to give rabbinic and ecclesial traditions of interpretation both the benefit of the doubt and the benefit of doubt: the former, by assuming that there are dimensions of scriptural meaning which are disclosed only by way of the hermeneutical practices of believing communities and believing traditions of Jews or Christians; the latter, by assuming, in the spirit of post-Spinozistic criticism, that these dimensions may be clarified through the disciplined practice of philological, historical and textual/rhetorical criticism"; Ochs, "Introduction to Postcritical," 3. For a summary of the approach, cf. Soulen and Soulen, *Handbook of Biblical Criticism*, 156–58.

interpretation.[10] At the same time, God reveals God's self to the world in and through Scripture, and we, the readers, are bound to wrestle with this: "You search the scriptures, because you think that in them you have eternal life; and it is they that bear witness to me" (John 5:39 RSV).

INTERPRETING WITHIN THE HORIZON OF THE CROSS

Jesus says that the Scriptures bear witness to him. It's right there in John 5. In fact, a bit farther on, Jesus says, "If you believed Moses, you would believe me, for he wrote about me. But if you do not believe what he wrote, how will you believe what I say?" (John 5:46–47) Modifying the text in line with chapter 2, "If you trusted Moses, you would trust me, for he wrote about me. But if you do not trust what he wrote, how will you trust what I say?" Scripture attributed to Moses witnesses to the trustworthiness of God revealed in Jesus Christ. While this is a mind-bender from the vantage of linear history, these statements from Jesus form this Christ-mystical disposition to Scripture: "All of Scripture everywhere deals only with Christ."[11] Such a claim only makes sense within the imagination of faith/trust in Jesus Christ, the eternal, incarnate, crucified, and risen Word.

So we have this Bible, which from a sociohistorical vantage point is a complex collection of texts compiled over the course of more than a millennium, reflecting different sources and streams of thought with an amalgam of theologies redacted into a whole that retains contradictions and maintains its tattered edges. The Bible itself reflects varied worldviews, not least of which is the fact that it reflects multiple major language worlds: primarily ancient Hebrew

---

10 I refer here to beneficial critiques and constructive insights of liberationist, feminist, womanist, and postcolonial interpreters—e.g., Reid, *Wisdom's Feast*; Yee, *Hebrew Bible*; Gafney, *Womanist Midrash*; Sugirtharah, *Bible and Asia*.

11 Luther, "Avoiding the Doctrines of Men" (1522), in *LW* 35.132.

and ancient Greek with a smattering of Aramaic, a sprinkling of Latin, and linguistic remnants of a variety of other Ancient Near Eastern languages. Glimpsing the complexity from the vantage of looking at the extremes, on one end of the hermeneutical spectrum, there is the idea that the Bible is verbally inspired, infallible, and inerrant, and on the other end of the spectrum, there is the idea that the Bible is a variegated collection of texts from a variety of Ancient Near Eastern cultures and contexts that reflect humans, primarily males, wrestling with God/gods. Writing about the Old Testament, Erhard Gerstenberger summarizes,

> The Old Testament cannot of itself offer any unitary theological or ethical view, since it is a conglomerate of experiences of faith from very different historical and social situations. Moreover the testimonies are very fragmentary; and they have been edited and manipulated very heavily before coming down to us. . . . I simply want to emphasize that I in no way regard the plurality and the clearly recognizable syncretism of the Old Testament tradition as a disaster, but as an extraordinary stroke of good fortune. The diversity of the theologies opens up for us a view of other peoples, times and ideas of God; it relieves us of any pressure to look anxiously for the one, unhistorical, immutable, absolutely obligatory notion and guideline in the ups and downs of histories and theologies. It frees us for the honest, relaxed assessment of the theological achievement of our spiritual forbears that they deserve, and it makes us capable, in dialogue with them and with the religions of the world, of finding and formulating the "right" faith in God, i.e. a faith to be expressed here and now, for an age which represents a turning point and perhaps an end.[12]

Gerstenberger's assessment reflects the disposition of much of contemporary Christian biblical scholarship. We look at the "faith" of

---

12 Gerstenberger, *Theologies in the Old Testament*, 1–2.

our forebears reflected in the text and sort out the "right" faith for today. The question of what the text as we receive it has to say about who the triune God is is of little interest, as the varied texts collected into the corpus called the Bible each reflect ages, cultures, and issues of bygone times. The imagination of faith does not ignore or disregard such sociocultural, historical information. Rather, the imagination of faith receives such information as penultimate and moves to the primary locus from which to view Scripture: the cross, a historical and cosmic event.

The basic benchmark for such a disposition comes in one of Luther's lesser-known hermeneutical teachings: *Crux Christi unica est eruditio verborum Dei, theologia sincerissima.*[13] That is, "the cross of Christ alone is the teaching of the word of God, the most genuine theology."[14] Given what we have explored to this point, this is fundamentally an exercise of the imagination of faith, a disposition that accompanies trusting in Jesus Christ. The imagination of faith reveals the world not with a set of rules but by means of an orientation to the fact that all Scripture exists within the interpretive horizon of Jesus Christ. That is, all Scripture (for Christians, the Old and New Testaments) is read and interpreted in and through Christ, in particular from the foot of the cross.

I expect that some will receive this as a flimsy hermeneutic. Too mystical. Perhaps. Remember, dear reader, that what I am suggesting is *not* a methodology. The imagination of faith is a disposition and one that is unapologetically Christocentric.[15] The Old Testament

13 From Luther's lecture on Psalm 6, WA 5.217, quoted in Oberman, *Luther*, 248.

14 Heaven knows that Luther, a person of his day (contextualizing but not excusing), was capable of making a mess of biblical interpretation, sometimes with lasting and disastrous consequences, especially with regard to the triune God's relationship with Jews. An example is his acerbic use of Scripture and invective being "Against the Jews and Their Lies" (1543), in *LW* 47.137–306. See also Oberman, *Roots of Anti-Semitism*; and Steigmann-Gall, *Holy Reich*.

15 As a biblical scholar, I have learned a great deal about this disposition from Jewish colleagues who call for and invite Christians to be true to the tradition of Christian interpretation. Jacob Neusner teaches that "while the world at large treats Judaism as 'the religion of the Old Testament,' the fact

makes sense *for Christians* only in relation to God's self-revelation in Jesus Christ. With not a little irony, Luther was spot-on. The cross of Christ is the teaching of the word of God, the most genuine theology. Such is the imagination of faith.

SOME INTERPRETIVE DIRECTION FROM JESUS

Jesus read and interpreted Scripture (e.g., Luke 4:16–30), the Word interpreting the written word.

Christian Scripture can be both beautiful and ugly. Not every text rolls as smoothly as "For God so loved the world." In tension with John 3:16 are texts like Joshua 11:20[16] and Ezekiel 20:11.[17] Nearly thirty years ago, Phyllis Trible published *Texts of Terror: Literary-Feminist Readings of Biblical Narratives*, in which she, a biblical scholar, exposed and explored biblical narratives of violence in particular texts that had contributed to violence against women.[18] Thanks to Professor Trible and now a host of others, we are more rightly aware of the terror and violence in some biblical texts and in some biblical interpretations. We cannot ignore or explain away such texts. Scripture is Scripture, which means, at least in part, that

---

is otherwise. Judaism inherits and makes the Hebrew Scriptures its own, just as does Christianity," quoted in Seitz, *Word without End*, 61–74. Similarly, Jon Levenson invites Christian interpreters to read the Hebrew Scriptures as Christians and not out of guilt or shame, warning that "Christians must ultimately aim for another sense as well, one that upholds the idea that their two-volume Bible is a meaningful whole, lest their scripture decompose before their very eyes"; Levenson, *Hebrew Bible*, 103. As Jews read Tanakh in relation to God's covenant with Israel, so Christians read the Old Testament in relation to God's self-revelation in Jesus Christ.

16 "For it was the Lord's doing to harden their hearts that they should come against Israel in battle, in order that they should be utterly destroyed, and should receive no mercy but be exterminated, as the Lord commanded Moses" (Josh 11:20 RSV).

17 "I gave them my statutes and showed them my ordinances, by whose observance man shall live" (Ezek 20:11 RSV).

18 Trible, *Texts of Terror.*

we are stuck with the good and the bad. Our challenge is to interpret them faithfully for today.

Reading with Jesus does not make all the problems inherent in the biblical text disappear. Reading with Jesus reframes Scripture in light of Jesus Christ himself, as is clear in the road to Emmaus story (Luke 24:27). Cleopas and the other disciple, after their eyes are opened, recall Jesus's interpretation of Scripture for them along the way (Luke 24:32). After they hightail it back to Jerusalem to share news of their experience on the road, the risen Lord appears to the disciples. Following a fish breakfast, Jesus "opened their minds to understand the scriptures" (Luke 24:45). It is clear in the latter half of Luke 24 that Jesus interprets Scripture in light of himself in a way that opens the disciples' eyes and minds.[19] At play here is that the written word is understood in and through the living Word, crucified and risen.

In John's Gospel, a similar dynamic comes into focus at the end of chapter 5. The story, which runs throughout the chapter, begins with a focus on a person sick for thirty years. He has been hanging out at the healing pool of Bethzatha, near the gate in the walls of Jerusalem called the Sheep Gate. His illness means that he was unable to get into the pool at the right time to be healed. (This bit of the story is wildly interesting, but in the interest of focus . . .) Jesus sees the fellow, and altogether foregoing the dip in the pool, Jesus heals him. All we hear are Jesus's words: "Rise, take up your mat, and walk." The guy, healed in the moment after decades of illness, takes up his mat and walks (John 5:8–9). Great. Lovely.

As if the healing itself is merely setting the scene for the point to come, the religious leaders of the day get in the face of this newly healed fellow: "It is the Sabbath; it is not lawful for you to carry your mat" (John 5:10). Missing the forest for the trees, one might think. The conversation turns to Jesus, as he is the one who healed and who commanded this guy to carry his mat, thereby breaking the

---

19 Similarly, in the synagogue in Nazareth, Jesus reads from the scroll of Isaiah (61:1, 2; 58:6) and says of the reading and the moment, "Today this scripture has been fulfilled in your hearing" (Luke 4:21).

Sabbath.[20] Who does he think he is? Exactly the point. What follows is a robust monologue in which Jesus speaks of his relationship with the Father. All that the Son is comes from the Father, including the Son's ability to speak on the Father's behalf with the Father's authority to bring life from death. The dust-up over the Sabbath builds to this revelation of the intimate relationship of Father and Son, ultimately culminating in Jesus teaching about the relationship of the Son to Scripture. Recall that the command to keep Sabbath is central to the biblical witness, built into the fabric of creation and of time (see Gen 1:1–2:3, especially 2:1–3). Keeping Sabbath, a "sign" of the covenant between God and God's people (Exod 31:12–17), meant resting as God rested.[21] No work. Yet this is exactly what Jesus has done.

As noted, the center of the monologue that follows is the relationship between Father and Son; in particular, what Jesus says and does is what the Father wills. In the end, Jesus turns to Scripture, saying,

> And the Father who sent me has himself borne witness to me. His voice you have never heard, his form you have never seen; and you do not have his word abiding in you, for you do not believe him whom he has sent. *You search the scriptures, because you think that in them you have eternal life; and it is they that bear witness to me*; yet you refuse to come to me that you may have life. . . . *If you believed Moses, you would believe me, for he wrote of me. But if you do not believe his writings, how will you believe my words?* (John 5:37–40, 46–47 RSV; emphases added)

Jesus leaves this scene with an interpretive paradox. Within the tradition, it is understood that Moses wrote the Torah, and in the Torah, it is abundantly clear that the Sabbath is to be kept and revered as a

---

20 The text suggests that this was not a one-off breaking of the Sabbath, as John 5:16b is better translated as the following: Jesus did these kinds of things on the Sabbath (ὅτι ταῦτα ἐποίει ἐν σαββάτῳ). It is also the case that there are other such stories in the Synoptic Gospels—e.g., Matthew, Mark, and Luke.

21 Also Exod 16:22–30; 20:8–11; Deut 5:12–15, passim.

blessing from God, a sign of the covenant. A central commandment. Yet Jesus not only broke the Sabbath but commanded another to do so as well. The conclusion of this episode has Jesus saying two key things. First, the Scriptures witness to him, the Eternal Son, the eternal Word incarnate. To be clear, he's speaking of the Hebrew Bible / Old Testament. Second and in Johannine fashion, faith/trust enters the picture. The final verses, for the purpose of this little book, might be better translated as "If you [trusted] Moses, you would [trust] me, for he wrote of me. But if you do not [trust] his writings, how will you [trust] my words?"

Heaven knows this does not rid Scripture of its interpretive challenges. It does, however, guide the imagination of faith. Scripture—the Old and New Testaments—witnesses first to Jesus Christ. As such, Jesus's encounter with the disciples on the way to Emmaus is about opening the Scriptures and opening their minds to read the Bible in light of Jesus Christ, the incarnate, crucified, and risen Word.

The implications of this do not require—and perhaps even resist—a method. Rather, interpreting Scripture is framed as an imaginative exercise from the disposition of trust in Jesus Christ. Scripture's witness to Jesus Christ, Lord and Savior, is paramount. Recall again the end of John 20: *These stories were written that you might trust and that in trusting, you might have life* (paraphrased). If it is in light of Jesus that we read Scripture, it is in light of the crucified and risen Lord. That is, the life that comes in and with trusting in Jesus does not come without suffering and death. It is resurrected life. This is not to justify texts that have caused and continue to cause harm in Scripture. It is to say that as Scripture, they are properly read in light of Jesus's incarnation, death, and resurrection.

Here's the kicker: Recall again *all things* in Colossians 1:15–20—in particular, that God reconciles "all things" to God's self through the blood of the cross. Consider that "all things" includes Scripture and that at times, we are called to critique texts in and through Jesus Christ.

In the Sermon on the Mount, there are a series of "you have heard it said, but I say" sayings, where Jesus critiques misinterpretations of Scripture. The culminating portion begins, "You have heard that it was said, 'You shall love your neighbor and hate your enemy.' But I say to you: Love your enemies and pray for those who persecute you" (Matt 5:43–44). Take this as an example of Jesus reading Scripture in light of himself, of *all things* being reconciled. He draws here on Leviticus 19:18b: "You shall love your neighbor as yourself." He is addressing a trend to interpret this text with a pretty clear fence around the definition of *neighbor. Neighbor* is not a term generally applied to everyone. The interpretive trend suggests that there are different rules for neighbors and enemies. Looking at the Holiness Code, the portion of Leviticus whence this well-known saying comes, tends to give credence to the trend: the enemy does not fare well—for example, "You shall chase your enemies, and they shall fall before you by the sword" (Lev 26:7 RSV).[22] So when Jesus says, "But I say to you, Love your enemies and pray for those who persecute you," this is a radical shift. This is Jesus reading Scripture in light of himself. And, I would argue, this is an example of the disposition toward Scripture that comes with the imagination of faith. Indeed, Jesus is redefining *enemy* in ways that we haven't even begun to imagine.[23]

---

22 The enemy is the enemy throughout Leviticus 26. As elsewhere, the enemy can be used by God as an instrument of punishment. Even with this, there is nothing near a command to love the enemy.

23 Throughout Psalms, enemies play a large role and present a challenge for many contemporary readers. I was chatting with a woman dying of cancer. I had read the psalm for the coming Sunday prior to our sharing Communion. As we chatted about the psalm, I shared my discomfort with the holy invective toward the enemy, naively expecting her to share the unease. She retorted, "Pastor, I have an enemy. It's cancer. And hope that Jesus whoops its ass." Touché. There are multiple ways to read the passage. Another take on enemies in Psalms comes from Bonhoeffer: "Even today I can believe God's love and forgive enemies only through the cross of Christ, through the carrying out of God's vengeance. The cross of Jesus applies to everyone"; Bonhoeffer, *Life Together*, 5:175–76.

ON PROCLAMATION

Trusting in Jesus is not our own doing. We cannot by our own gumption just muster faith within us. This is not how trust is kindled. Hearing the gospel of Jesus Christ—the trustworthiness of God—is the means by which the Spirit moves the heart to trust in Jesus Christ.[24] In this hearing, the imagination is reconciled from trusting in that which is not God to trust in God, from death to life. As the Spirit nurtures "ears to hear,"[25] the world as it is in Jesus Christ is opened by way of the imagination of faith. Our trust in Jesus being as fickle as it is, hearing the gospel is not a one-and-done deal. The individual benefits from regularly being encountered by the living Word, the trustworthiness of God.

The main purpose of the church is stewarding the proclamation of the gospel of Jesus Christ *with the sole purpose of nurturing trust in Jesus Christ, which will open the world anew.* The proclamation of the Word is at the heart of what the church is, and clarity about this purpose is paramount.[26] When the church loses this focus, dry rot spreads from pulpit to pew. The church might look like the church, but without clarity about the gospel, the whole of the church becomes brittle, often without us even knowing it. Preaching a gospel other than the gospel of Jesus Christ is ultimately dangerous, as it locates trust and hope in that which is not Jesus Christ.

---

24 Martin Luther on the Apostles' Creed, article III: "I believe that by my own understanding or strength I cannot believe in Jesus Christ my Lord or come to him, but instead the Holy Spirit has called me through the gospel, enlightened me with his gifts, made me holy and kept me in the true faith, just as he calls, gathers, enlightens, and makes holy the whole Christian church on earth and keeps it with Jesus Christ in the one common, true faith"; *BC* 355–56.6.

25 The Hebrew prophets regularly say, "Hear the word of the Lord"—e.g., Isa 1:10. It is of course possible to have one's ears open and not hear what is said—e.g., Isa 42:20; Jer 5:21. The Lord, via Isaiah, opens ears to new things—e.g., Isa 48:6. Jesus draws upon Isaiah in Matt 15:16.

26 E.g., from Melanchthon's "Augsburg Confession" (1530), article VII—"It is also taught that at all times there must be and remain one holy, Christian church. It is the assembly of all believers among whom the gospel is purely preached and the holy sacraments are administered according to the gospel"; *BC* 42.1.

The health of the church's proclamation—that is, what makes a sermon good—is determined by one central thing: the preaching of the crucified and risen Christ, the trustworthiness of God, as the ultimate truth of the sinner and of the cosmos. Idols, whether little statues or dollar signs or even the most well-meaning ideology, are not the gospel of Jesus Christ. To preach as if these idols are more powerful than Jesus Christ is faithless. Does this sound too harsh? Perhaps it does. It is not, however. There is no hope in worshipping ourselves. Faith creates a new reality. Faith creates and unleashes a freedom that has great potential for good, for transformation, for freedom to be with and for the other for the sake of the common good.

WHAT IS THE SERMON FOR?

As someone who grew up in the church and really did not like listening to sermons (still don't!), I might say the sermon is a great time for a nap. It's biblical. Remember Eutychus, the fellow who nodded off while Paul was preaching, fell out a third-story window, and died (Acts 20:7–12)?[27] I have nodded off during a sermon or two, and I've watched as others have nodded off while I've been preaching. While a nap might be a peripheral benefit for the really tired, it is not the main point.

The main point of the sermon *every single time* is the trustworthiness of God. As discussed earlier, this comes from the Scriptures read in and through Jesus Christ. This trustworthiness looks like a cross whose roots and branches envelop the whole of the cosmos, upon which hang all the sins of the world, upon which Christ took on these sins and our death, gifting the cosmos with His righteousness, freedom, and life. The cross of Christ is the tree of life. Trusting in Jesus invites us to see the world in this way—enveloped by this life-giving

27 Whether Eutychus died or not is a bit unclear. He ended up alive by the end of the story, but he missed the sermon.

tree.[28] The point of the sermon is to invite the hearer to find their life and the life of the world in this cruciform tree of life. Nothing exists outside the reconciling scope of Christ's crucifixion, by which God reconciles *all things* to God's self (Col 1:15–20). Likewise, all things are interrelated. We exist in relation with all people, all of creation, the whole of the cosmos. Trust that this is indeed true, even fleeting trust, is the lifeblood of the imagination of faith, opening the world *as it is in Christ Jesus.*

Notice that, as was discussed about the interpretation of Scripture, this is a disposition, not a method. There are a million different ways to structure the sermon, but the point is always the same: the cosmos has been reconciled by God through the cross of Jesus Christ, and this reconciliation includes you, the hearer, as well as your neighbor and your enemy. The sermon promises that this trustworthiness of God is true even though it is often not immediately apparent. Our propensity to trust in that which is not God, which we live with throughout our lives, always needs to be met week after week with the promise of God's trustworthiness.[29] While "all things" have been reconciled, our imaginations are in continual need of being formed to this reconciliation, being reformed toward freedom in Jesus Christ. Faith is an end in itself (Eph 2:8). And faith reveals that Jesus is life for one's self, for the neighbor, for the enemy, for the world.

A challenge here is that the gospel is not and cannot be an imperative. It is an invitation. Imperatives are far easier to offer from the pulpit. Do this. Don't do that. Behave this way and not that. Yet this turns the gospel into another law, shifting the focus back to ourselves and away from Jesus. When we attempt salvation by following the law (*corum Deo* / before God, here), we always inevitably end up

28 I draw here upon the vision of the cross as the world tree from Christianity in Nordic lands, where the inherited vision of Yggdrasil, the great ash tree that enveloped the cosmos, became associated with the cross of Christ; cf. Murphy, *Tree of Salvation*. See also Giere, "Practice of Being Rooted," 317–21.

29 Recall "I believe; help my unbelief!" (Mark 9:24). Consider I trust; help my lack of trust or distrust or mistrust.

worshipping ourselves, our ability to obey. Upon those who fail, including ourselves, judgment is unleashed rather than love.

SO WHAT OF SIN?

Everyone is curious about sin. Sin is interesting. Sin sells! But what about the place of sin in preaching? How does sin play with the imagination of faith?

First of all, sin, as idolatry, is real. So often, sin gets reduced to what one does with their tingly bits or a breach of someone's morality. Considering sin as idolatry (trusting in that which is not God) is far more important, as it has to do with faith.

Preachers and hearers are all idolaters. All of us. No one is exempt from misplaced trust. "All have sinned and fallen short," says Paul.[30] So should the preacher thrash their hearers with this knowledge as if the awareness of sin is the church's cudgel? No. The preacher should not and ought not to beat the hearer with such knowledge, leaving open wounds to be covered with a superficial Jesus bandage. This is not love. This is not sharing the Word, in whom there is life. This is driving the hearer away from life, away from freedom. While such a cudgel might be effective, as obedience can be coerced through any number of means, obedience is not the point of the gospel of Jesus Christ. Cowering, one might think, "If only I could get my shit together." This directs the person to their own ability or inability rather than to Christ's mercy and love,

---

30 "But now, apart from the law, the righteousness of God has been disclosed and is attested by the Law and the Prophets, the righteousness of God through [trust in] Jesus Christ for all who [trust]. *For there is no distinction, since all have sinned and fall short of the glory of God*; they are now justified by his grace as a gift, through the redemption that is in Christ Jesus, whom God put forward as a sacrifice of atonement by his blood, effective through [trust]. He did this to demonstrate his righteousness, because in his divine forbearance he had passed over the sins previously committed; it was to demonstrate at the present time his own righteousness, so that he is righteous and he justifies the one who [trusts in] Jesus" (Rom 3:21–26; emphases added).

which has already been given in spite of the person's sin (Rom 5:8). For those who rightly refuse to cower at such a cudgel, it divorces the power of life from their lives. Such wielding of the power of the gospel is contrary to the news that is good, contrary to Jesus Christ.

Should the sermon avoid this misplaced trust then? Absolutely not. As opposed to wielding the knowledge of sin as a cudgel, the role of sin in preaching is descriptive. Recall that there is a thin line between sin (trusting in that which is not God) and faith (trusting in Jesus Christ). Sin's role in the sermon is that it reflects the reality in which we live, the reality of the world. Whenever we trust in that which is not God, we sin. When we seek life from that which cannot give life, we sin. Golden calves come in all shapes and sizes. When we displace Jesus as Lord and Savior, most often in favor of ourselves or an ideology that replaces the gospel, we sin. When we disregard the reflection of the divine in each and every human being on the planet, we sin. Recall the warning of the psalmist regarding the idol: "Those who make them are like them; so are all who trust in them" (Ps 115:8). The gospel of Jesus Christ calls us forward into life, which goes hand in hand with trusting in Jesus. Hence the role of sin in the sermon is an accurate description of reality, a mirror of existence,[31] insofar as reality includes trusting in that which is not God accompanied by the promise that nothing can "separate us from the love of God in Christ Jesus our Lord."[32] This radical promise of God's trustworthiness invites the sermon to serve as a mirror of reality that takes sin seriously. Sin is not fictitious, and neither can the mercy and grace of God in Jesus Christ be fictitious. Neither are we fictitious sinners. Sin is real, and we are real sinners.[33] The cross

31 See Herman Stuempfle's description of Paul Tillich's formulation of the law as a "mirror of existence"; Stuempfle, *Preaching Law and Gospel*, 23–32.

32 More fully, "For I am convinced that neither death, nor life, nor angels, nor rulers, nor things present, nor things to come, nor powers, nor height, nor depth, nor anything else in all creation will be able to separate us from the love of God in Christ Jesus our Lord" (Rom 8:38–39).

33 At the close of a letter to his pal and fellow reformer Philip Melanchthon on August 1, 1521, Luther wrote, "If you are a preacher of grace, then preach a true and not a fictitious grace; if grace is true, you must bear a true and not

frees us to look deeply and honestly at the reality of our idols and the consequences of our idolatry because God's love incarnate in Jesus Christ is more powerful, and the mercy and grace of God are the world's ultimate reality.

As such, providing that we are clear about the gospel of Jesus Christ, naming our common human reality of trusting in that which is not God opens the way for a clearer vision of the mysteries of heaven and the open secret that is the love of God incarnate, crucified and risen for the life of the world. This is the open secret of the imagination of faith: in spite of what our senses tell us, the world has been redeemed in Jesus Christ.

SERMON AS ART

The sermon, as the weekly narration of the trustworthiness of the triune God, is a perpetual exercise of invitation into the world revealed in Christ. This is a world in need of the reconciliation that it has already been given. Drawing people into this truth is an artistic movement, as art can see the world as it is and as it might be. Given the proleptic (already–not yet) nature of God's reconciling movement in Jesus Christ, the sermon as art sees the world as it is and as it is not. In art there is the freedom to explore honestly death and life, to explore the world, which God declared "very good" and which also has its wounds and scars. Art can reveal the vile reality that

---

a fictitious sin. God does not save people who are only fictitious sinners. Be a sinner and sin boldly, but believe and rejoice in Christ even more boldly, for he is victorious over sin, death, and the world. As long as we are here [in this world] we have to sin. This life is not the dwelling place of righteousness, but, as Peter says, we look for new heavens and a new earth in which righteousness dwells. It is enough that by the riches of God's glory we have come to know the Lamb that takes away the sin of the world. No sin will separate us from the Lamb, even though we commit fornication and murder a thousand times a day. Do you think that the purchase price that was paid for the redemption of our sins by so great a Lamb is too small? Pray boldly—you too are a mighty sinner"; *LW* 48.281–82.

we desperately want to ignore, and it can reintroduce domesticated wonder to the wilds of the world. In the words of Trevor Hart, "The artistic imagination ventures forth, as it were, into a world believed to be already rich with actual and potential meaning, lays hold of materials whose natural qualities encourage some modes of handling and resist others, and, through a creative exchange with all this, renders the fruits of its interpretative labours into form for the benefit of those who, as yet, lack the eyes to see and ears to hear."[34] While not Professor Hart's subject here, he describes the art of preaching. Art as art has the power to stoke the imagination about what is and what might be. The sermon as art has the power by the movement of the Spirit to stoke the imagination of faith in those captive to the imagination of death. The sermon as art creatively invites people to embrace that they, along with their sin and their death, have been taken into Christ himself as the cosmic reconciliation of *all things*. Not only that, but the sermon of Jesus as the cosmic Christ invites the hearer to embrace that this is also true for their neighbor, their enemy, and the whole of the cosmos. Hence the work of preaching is more akin to the movements of poetry, dance, and music than to logic. As with the liturgy and sacraments that accompany the proclamation, the sermon is art through which the Word reveals the world as it is in Christ.

Such radical imagination, of course, proceeds from trusting in Jesus Christ, who is the incarnate trustworthiness of God. The preacher's disposition toward this sermon as art is necessarily Christocentric and cruciform. God's trustworthiness is not an abstract but the person of Jesus Christ. As a means of grounding the imagination of faith *of the preacher* in this work, consider Bonhoeffer's description of the sermon: "The proclaimed word is the incarnate Christ himself. . . . The proclaimed word is not a medium of expression for something else, something which lies behind it, but rather it is the Christ himself walking through the congregation as the Word."[35]

34 Hart, "Through the Arts," 9.

35 From Bonhoeffer's lectures on homiletics, as found in Bonhoeffer and Fant, *Bonhoeffer*, 126.

Christ himself is present and active as the incarnate, crucified, and risen Word in, with, and under the ordinary words of the sermon, instilling and inviting by the power of the Spirit trust/faith. As Paul says, "Faith comes from what is heard, and what is heard comes by the preaching of Christ" (Rom 10:17 RSV). In this sense, it is Christ himself who meets the hearer in the midst of their here and now, promises to the hearer the trustworthiness of God, and invites the hearer to see and to hear and to move and to feel and to smell with the imagination of faith.

Such a faith-oriented conception of preaching invites a great deal of creative leeway as long as the center and purpose remain clear. The gospel is the story of God's trustworthiness. Recall the three-legged stool of freedom in faith: Freedom from the power of sin and death. Recognizing God as God. The unification of the believer with Christ. While there are things that flow from trusting in Jesus, trusting in Jesus is an end in itself. It is the justification of the sinner. It is the defeat of death's power. It is becoming one with Christ. It is revealing the world as it is in Jesus Christ, which impacts how we abide in this reconciled and yet unreconciled world, where sin and death remain real.

ON BEING

As we have seen, imagination, common to all humans, has a good deal to do with how we navigate life, how we narrate our story in relation to the story of the world. The imagination of faith frees us from ignoring the world's suffering, injustice, and death because on the cross, God revealed God's commitment to the whole world. On the cross, Jesus revealed God's commitment to the world in a way that minimizing does not necessitate any of the world's suffering. The all-embracing branches of this cruciform tree of life embrace and reconcile the whole.

So what? What's the payoff? Does any of this trust and imagination business better the world? What about discipleship? Remember that in the book of James, it is written that "faith by itself, if it has no works, is dead" (Jas 2:17 RSV). These are all pertinent and fine questions, but they often either assume or leapfrog over trusting in Jesus to a fixation on Christian behavior or even the reduction of Christianity to a moralism. Perhaps for the sake of one last provocation, too much concern about the payoff of faith is itself faithless.

Consider that discipleship is also a disposition of the imagination of faith—an invitation to see the world as it is in Christ. To get there, first consider that imagination can fail. Like other aspects of being human, imagination can go astray or break down.

FAILURE OF IMAGINATION

Imagination, like the rest of us, is susceptible to failure. Unlike a knee or a hip, however, we have not sorted out how to put in a new synthetic imagination so that when failure of the imagination happens, it can be replaced or rebooted. As the imagination is one of the remaining frontiers of the mind, it is a complex matrix of cause and effect, of neural relationships, of the interpretation of memory (internal) and the world (external).[36] While rooted in the simplicity of language, imagination, which is central to each and every human being, is wildly complex.

For our purposes, it is important that we keep in mind that the imagination is a central and complex aspect of being human, that the imagination needs to be nurtured, and that it is by way of the imagination that we understand who we are and what life means. It is just as critical that we understand that there is such a thing as the failure of imagination. Whether in adults or children (recall William Golding's *Lord of the Flies*), the imagination can be conformed to the nefarious and fearful as much as to love. While there is a value in imagination for imagination's sake, there is also the reality that imagination can break, fail, and lead to dark places. Recall that from

36 Byrne, *Rational Imagination*, xi.

the vantage of neuroscience, "the mind/brain does not represent or mirror reality; it *constructs* a virtual reality of its own."[37] When this construction of a virtual reality, which is common to each and every human being on the planet, squirts out sideways, you end up with more mustard on your shirt than your hot dog. Imagination is as susceptible to pathology as skin cells and relationships are.

There are obvious maladies of brain chemistry or of brain trauma that result in pathologies of the imagination. For example, hallucinations (sensory in character) and delusions (disjointed understandings of belief or meaning) are both maladies of the imagination.[38] When I was a teenager, my appendix burst. It was taken out. Accompanying the successful appendectomy was a serious trip under the influence of anesthesia and a serious infection from the little bugger bursting. For a couple of days postsurgery, I saw with my own two eyes pink elephants and trains moving through my hospital room. As a side effect of the anesthesia in concert with the infection, my brain chemistry ended up a mess. I was hallucinating. Tripping, if you like. My imagination, while entertaining to me, was out of whack.

In contrast, a bit later in life, I had the opportunity to serve as a chaplain in an institution that served people with drug and alcohol addiction and extreme mental illness. It was regular to have folks admitted for detoxification. One such patient, upon admission, was convinced that they were someone other than who they were. "I am Jesus fucking Christ, and I have the strength of a thousand fucking bears!" they shouted repeatedly with confidence. While there may have been hallucinations involved, this individual was delusional. While I believe that Jesus Christ will return as we confess in the Nicene Creed, this person was in a drug- and alcohol-induced delusion. When their brain chemistry stabilized, they became quite clear that while both strong and pious, their earlier claims resulted from their imagination being on drugs.

37 Modell, *Imagination and the Meaningful Brain*, 13.

38 Cf. Davies, *Imagination*, especially chap. 5.

When imaginations are disordered by imbalanced chemistry and/or trauma, our modern medicine seeks to treat the condition therapeutically. There is a relatively new openness to addressing such challenges as addiction and brain health, often tangled together, and there is much to be thankful for in terms of these treatments, but we have a great distance yet to go in terms of reducing public stigma.

While such physiological maladies and chemical imbalances can result in failures of imagination—perhaps either "fractures" or "distortions" of imagination is a better description—for the purpose of this book, "failure of imagination" is everyday and insidious. In his novel *The Power and the Glory* (1940), English writer Graham Greene uses the term *failure of imagination* in precisely this everyday, insidious way. While Greene's writing was popular in his day, it is unfair to you, dear reader, to assume a *Harry Potter* level of popular awareness about Greene's work today. So by way of introduction, the protagonist of the novel is a Roman Catholic priest. He is not named but identified with the moniker "the whisky priest." This is a nod toward his waywardness, of which he is deeply aware and about which others are happy to remind him. The priest, in his brokenness, is on a journey of discovery as he peels back layers of his own judgmentalism en route to a place of accepting others with their flaws, even if he never reaches such acceptance of himself. The setting is a fictional state in Mexico, where religion and liquor have been outlawed.

The whisky priest, for all his foibles, is on the run from the authorities because he refuses to renounce his faith. Betrayed by a companion, a Judas-like character, the priest is apprehended because he has some brandy on his person. While in jail, he ends up chatting with his cellmates, which include a "pious woman" who is particularly offended by a couple copulating in the corner of the cell. Her judgment of them is relentless. As she pushes the priest to do something about it, the priest shares with her a bit of his clarity: "When you visualized a man or woman carefully, you could always begin to feel pity—that was a quality God's image carried with it. When you saw the lines at the corners of the eyes, the shape of the mouth, how the hair grew, it was impossible to hate. Hate was just a failure of imagination."[39] The whisky priest comes to a point of clarity, specifically that hate is a spanner in the proper working of the imagination. In this case, hate impedes the imagination from recognizing the image of God in the other, whoever they are and whatever they've done. Such failure of imagination clouds the imagination's vision with hate and yields judgment, whereas the imagination of faith "sees" the image of God in each person, yielding pity, mercy, and love. The whisky priest, an obviously imperfect character, remains faithful to who God revealed God's self to be, as we hear in Jesus's words from the cross: "Father, forgive them; for they know not what they do" (Luke 23:34 RSV). This hate causes the failure of the imagination and impairs clear vision like a faithless cataract.

We are beings whose imaginations are formed from perhaps the earliest days of our lives. We live within a pastiche of narratives in which we are the main character. Some of the threads are wholesome; some, not so much. We are always in the process of narrating our life stories, weaving threads into ever-emerging tapestries that are who we imagine ourselves to be.

While we have agency in the workings of our imagination, this agency is not complete. Some threads of the story are programmed into our genetic code or worn into our gray matter. Many life stories include scars left by trauma. Whether abuse or war, traumatic narratives can leave deep ruts in the stories that are our lives, narratives that can clog or derail the imagination. Similarly, our personal narratives can conform to those who have a formative impact on us early in life. In so many ways, we learn by imitation, by repeating what we hear others say and what we see others do.[40]

---

39 Greene, *Power and the Glory*, 52.

40 Recall the insight of Rodgers and Hammerstein's "You've Got to Be Carefully Taught" from the musical *South Pacific*:

> You've got to be taught to hate and fear,
> You've got to be taught from year to year,
> It's got to be drummed in your dear little ear—
> You've got to be carefully taught!

If Modell is on track when he says that "the mind/brain does not represent or mirror reality; it *constructs* a virtual reality of its own,"[41] these collected stories are the material from which the brain constructs reality. Consider the stories that form your imagination about the world, the cosmos, the neighbor, the enemy. The gospel of Jesus Christ invites us into a particular narrative about the world already reconciled. Hate of any kind runs contrary to the narrative of Jesus Christ. Similarly, apathy of any kind runs contrary.

IMAGINATION OF FAITH, EMPATHY, AND LOVE

If Christ died for the helpless, the sinner, and the enemy, there is no one beyond God's reconciling movement of the cross.[42] Thank God, as this is God's trustworthiness. While there are many texts that speak of various aspects of Christian living, God does not promise the perfection of sinners.[43] God promises reconciliation to sinners in

---

You've got to be taught to be afraid
Of people whose eyes are oddly made,
And people whose skin is a different shade—
You've got to be carefully taught.

You've got to be taught before it's too late,
Before you are six or seven or eight,
To hate all the people your relatives hate—
You've got to be carefully taught!

Joshua Logan, dir. *South Pacific* (Los Angeles, CA: 20th Century Fox, 1958).

41 Modell, *Imagination and the Meaningful Brain*, 13.

42 See Rom 5:6–11.

43 The hope of the sinner—that is, the one who puts their trust in that which is not God . . . all of us—is Christ who is without sin (e.g., 2 Cor 5:21; 1 Pet 1:18–19; 1 John 3:5), who takes the world's sin upon himself and grants the sinner his righteousness. Luther, commenting on Galatians 3:13, illustrates the point: "Now let us see how two such extremely contrary things come together in this Person. Not only my sins and yours, but the sins of the entire world, past, present, and future, attack Him, try to damn Him, and do in fact damn Him. But because in the same Person, who is the highest, the greatest,

and through Christ. Perfection is not the goal. Faith, which is trust, in Jesus Christ is the goal, by the power of the Spirit.

Can we work on not being assholes to one another? Yes. Can we work on not treating one another as means to our own ends—as "Its"? Sure thing. Can we work on the continual adjustment of laws and systems in favor of the good of the individual and the common good of all, especially those without voice and power? You betcha. Can we work toward preserving the earth in all her beauty and splendor for generations to come? Absolutely. All this said, God does not promise this. Rather, God bids us to faith and promises that in faith, there is life abundant. Faith in Jesus Christ means freedom from the power of sin and death and the freedom for abundant life. The imagination of death encourages fear and division. The imagination of faith invites love.

As mentioned earlier, Bonhoeffer, in his book *Life Together*, captured a central aspect of the reconciled imagination as it relates to Christian being: "A Christian comes to others only through Jesus Christ."[44] While Bonhoeffer does not use the language of the reconciled imagination, the idea here is clear. The antidote to failed imagination is trusting in—that is, *being in*—Jesus Christ so that anyone or anything is encountered in and through the person and work of the cosmic Christ, the scope of whose mercy and love knows

---

and the only sinner, there is also eternal and invincible righteousness, therefore these two converge: the highest, the greatest, and the only sin; and the highest, the greatest, and the only righteousness. Here one of them must yield and be conquered, since they come together and collide with such a powerful impact. Thus the sin of the entire world attacks righteousness with the greatest possible impact and fury. What happens? Righteousness is eternal, immortal, and invincible. Sin, too, is a very powerful and cruel tyrant, dominating and ruling over the whole world, capturing and enslaving all men. In short, sin is a great and powerful god who devours the whole human race, all the learned, holy, powerful, wise, and unlearned men. He, I say, attacks Christ and wants to devour Him as he has devoured all the rest. But he does not see that He is a Person of invincible and eternal righteousness. In this duel, therefore, it is necessary for sin to be conquered and killed, and for righteousness to prevail and live. Thus in Christ all sin is conquered, killed, and buried; and righteousness remains the victor and the ruler eternally"; *LW* 26.280–81.

44 Bonhoeffer, *Life Together*, 5:31.

no bounds. The imagination of faith yields empathy; empathy forms our disposition to the other in light of Christ, who prayed for those crucifying him: "Father, forgive them; for they know not what they do" (Luke 23:34 RSV). This cruciform empathy makes a way for love. The imagination of faith invites us into the world as it is in Christ, which turns us out toward the world with renewed vision:

> From now on, therefore, we regard no one from a human point of view; even though we once knew Christ from a human point of view, we no longer know him in that way. So if anyone is in Christ, there is a new creation: everything old has passed away; look, new things have come into being! All this is from God, who reconciled us to himself through Christ and has given us the ministry of reconciliation; that is, in Christ God was reconciling the world to himself, not counting their trespasses against them, and entrusting the message of reconciliation to us. So we are ambassadors for Christ, since God is making his appeal through us; we entreat you on behalf of Christ: be reconciled to God. For our sake God made the one who knew no sin to be sin, so that in him we might become the righteousness of God. (2 Cor 5:16–21)

This is good faith: trust within which God bends our knowing and our vision of Christ, of one another, and of the world to Christ himself, the promised new creation. Such is the reconciliation of the imagination, given that we still live with at least one foot in the old creation.

Note that reconciliation is not intended to be an obscure matter, an answer in some pub trivia night. It is meant to be shared, to be known, to be trusted, to be lived in, to be lived out of. This message of personal and cosmic reconciliation has been entrusted to us for the sake of the world. In a world where the cultivation of division has become a commonplace strategy in the politics of parties and nations, this message of reconciliation—this invitation to the imagination of faith, which knows and sees in light of the new creation in Christ—is a countercultural gift to the world.

The message of this reconciliation is the call of the church, inviting others into the wondrous reconciliation that is Christ Jesus, that is new creation. The imagination of faith and the freedom in Christ accompany the message of reconciliation. From this freedom flow empathy and love for self, neighbor, and enemy because the identity, worth, and truth of everyone and everything are located in Christ. Within this freedom, there is both tenderness and power, as faith freed from the shackles of fear and death flows forth in love (Gal 5:6).

The ministry of reconciliation of which Paul speaks in 2 Corinthians is best understood as the reconciliation of the imagination to Christ Jesus. In Christ, we regard no one from a human point of view, even when all indications say otherwise. This is the reconciled imagination at work, inviting empathy and freeing the individual trusting in Jesus for love in a world preoccupied with fear and death.

DISCIPLESHIP AND DITCH DAISIES

I started this book with a description of the current dry rot in the church: the tendency to place our trust in that which is not God (bad faith) as opposed to trusting in Jesus Christ (good faith). Central to this is the current fixation in the church on both left and right ideologies rather than on the cosmic Christ, the incarnate, crucified, and living Word. Such bad faith regularly leads to trusting in one's self and boasting about what we do. It is my experience that this tendency is often called discipleship. But for this discipleship, Jesus is an example rather than the Lord and Savior, and as such, it is a distortion of both Christ and discipleship.[45]

45 Luther commenting on Gal 5:8: "Scripture presents Christ in two ways. First, as a gift. If I take hold of Him this way, I shall lack nothing whatever. 'In Christ are hid all the treasures of wisdom and knowledge' (Col. 2:3). As great as He is, He has been made by God my wisdom, righteousness, sanctification, and redemption (1 Cor. 1:30). Therefore even if I have committed many great sins, nevertheless, if I believe in Him, they are all swallowed up by His righteousness. Secondly, Scripture presents Him as an example for us to imitate. But I will not let this Christ be presented to me as exemplar except at a time of rejoicing,

Consider instead centering discipleship, the activity of faith, as holy wonder, the expression of the imagination of faith. Let's turn again to the Sermon on the Mount in order to consider the lilies:[46]

> "No one can serve two masters, for a slave will either hate the one and love the other or be devoted to the one and despise the other. You cannot serve God and wealth.
>
> "Therefore I tell you, do not worry about your life, what you will eat or what you will drink, or about your body, what you will wear. Is not life more than food and the body more than clothing? Look at the birds of the air: they neither sow nor reap nor gather into barns, and yet your heavenly Father feeds them. Are you not of more value than they? And which of you by worrying can add a single hour to your span of life? And why do you worry about clothing? Consider the lilies of the field, how they grow; they neither toil nor spin, yet I tell you, even Solomon in all his glory was not clothed like one of these. But if God so clothes the grass of the field, which is alive today and tomorrow is thrown into the oven, will he not much more clothe you—you of little faith? Therefore do not worry, saying, 'What will we eat?' or 'What will we drink?' or 'What will we wear?' For it is the gentiles who seek all these things, and indeed your heavenly Father knows that you need all these things. But seek first the kingdom of God and his righteousness, and all these things will be given to you as well.

---

when I am out of reach of temptations (when I can hardly attain a thousandth part of His example), so that I may have a mirror in which to contemplate how much I am still lacking, lest I become smug. But in a time of tribulation I will not listen to or accept Christ except as a gift, as Him who died for my sins, who has bestowed His righteousness on me, and who accomplished and fulfilled what is lacking in my life. For He 'is the end of the Law, that everyone who has faith may be justified' (Rom. 10:4)"; *LW* 27.34.

46 I am grateful to friend, theologian, and George MacDonald scholar Kirstin Jeffrey Johnson for drawing my attention to Jesus's command to consider the lilies.

> "So do not worry about tomorrow, for tomorrow will bring worries of its own. Today's trouble is enough for today." (Matt 6:24–34)

There are two movements in this text that undergird Jesus's framing of discipleship as a disposition of the imagination of faith.

The first is Jesus warning about the divided self: "No one can serve two masters" (Matt 6:24). To some degree, this is a Matthean reconfiguration of the first commandment—"You shall have no other gods before me" (Exod 20:3)—with echoes also of the Shema: "Hear, O Israel: the Lord our God is one Lord; and you shall love the Lord your God with all your heart, and with all your soul, and with all your might" (Deut 6:4–5 RSV). As the Lord is one, so too is the human being created in the Lord's image one. Human beings are most fully the humans we are created to be when we are of one allegiance. When our trust is not divided. As Jesus teaches, "No one can serve two masters. . . . You cannot serve God and mammon" (Matt 6:24 RSV). The Aramaic word *mammon* (מָמוֹן) often means money, cash, bling, but consider that *mammon* is the golden calf in one of its many guises. As such, *mammon* can be interpreted as any of these many golden calves that, though untrustworthy, demand our trust.

While Jesus is pretty clear with his warning about split devotion, truth be told, this is how we live, whether a person of faith or not. Yes, here I'm relying on Luther's theological understanding that the Christian is *sempre simul iustus et peccator*—that is, always simultaneously saint and sinner.[47] While we do live with split devotions, trusting in

47 In his "Summary of the Psalms" (1531), Luther introduced Psalm 32 as "an exemplary psalm of instruction that teaches us what sin is, and how one might be freed from it and be righteous before God. Our reason does not know what sin is and tries to make satisfaction for it with works. But the psalmist says that even saints are sinners. They cannot become holy or blessed except by confessing themselves as sinners before God, knowing that they are regarded as righteous only from the grace of God, apart from any service or work. In short, our righteousness is called (in plain language) the forgiveness of sins. Or, as it says here: 'sins not counted,' 'sins covered,' 'sins not to be seen.' Here stand the clear plain words: All the saints are sinners and remain sinners. But

both God and that which is not God, the grace and mercy of God cover the whole. This does not excuse the split devotion but rather turns our gaze to the cross, where Christ, by his death, reconciles sinners to God.

The second move can be characterized as somewhere between "Jesus fails pastoral care" and "Jesus calls people to be." Jesus's warning about the divided self flows naturally into a warning about anxiety. "Do not be anxious about your life," he says (Matt 6:25 RSV). Easy for Jesus to say, eh? This movement of his teaching ends with, "So do not worry about tomorrow, for tomorrow will bring worries of its own. Today's trouble is enough for today" (Matt 6:34). Perhaps not surprisingly, I prefer my own rendering: "So don't fret about tomorrow, for tomorrow will fret for itself. Sufficient for today is its own shit." There is a realness to Jesus's words here. Literally and figuratively, shit happens. Trusting in Jesus does not take this away. Is it a flaw of the universe? I don't think so. It is simply not scriptural to think that shit in all its many and various forms is not part of the world we live in. Remember, we live within the horizon of death. Perhaps outside of the eschatological vision of the new heavens and new earth (Rev 21:1–8), any vision of this world that is without pain, suffering, brokenness, struggle, or death has no traction in reality. It turns out that we and the world that we inhabit have *caca*: "Sufficient for the day is its own shit" (ἀρκετὸν τῇ ἡμέρᾳ ἡ κακία αὐτῆς). Expect it. Own it. We do not need to like it, but it is part and parcel of life on earth and the life of the cosmos. There's a good reason why passing through death resonates within and beyond the church.

Also on worry, Jesus says, "Do not worry about your life, what you will eat or what you will drink, or about your body, what you

---

they are holy because God in His grace neither sees nor counts these sins, but forgets, forgives, and covers them. There is thus no distinction between saints and the non-saints. They are sinners alike and all sin daily, only that the sins of the holy are not counted but covered; and the sins of the unholy are not covered but counted. One would have a healing dressing on and is bandaged; the other wound is open and undressed. Nevertheless, both of them are truly wounded, truly sinners, concerning which we in our books and in other places have abundantly bore witness"; Luther, *Reading the Psalms*, 67. Cf. WA 38.28.

will wear" (Matt 6:25). Again, easy for Jesus to say. And yet, while not easy, this is timely.

According to a report by the Kaiser Family Foundation published on February 10, 2021, the impact of the global pandemic on mental health, particularly anxiety and depression, is remarkable.[48] From the first half of 2019 to January 2021, the number of people suffering from anxiety and/or depression rose fourfold, with over 40 percent of households reporting at least one adult with anxiety and/or depression. Not to get bogged down in statistics, as they only tell a portion of the story, but the same study also shows that the impact on those under fifty—in particular, the eighteen- to twenty-four-year-old demographic, is way out of whack. What we are talking about here is a long-term impact on the mental health of many and, in particular, on the generation that is now entering adulthood. While this is due to the Covid-19 pandemic, many (especially those serving in ministry) will be aware of the plethora of causes for the hidden mental health pandemic within the pandemic. Global health, the health of the globe, and the deep and acrimonious crevices of political division have real impacts on the lives of real people, though often outwardly hidden, manifesting as depression and anxiety.

Jesus saying "Don't worry about your life" is not a cure-all. From my experience, the last thing one should say to someone having an anxiety attack is, "Chill out. Don't worry about your life." Jesus's words do, however, help extend the imagination of faith to life. In this portion of the text, it is also helpful to tend to how Jesus orients us toward time. The now is paramount. Moments beyond the now are always promise. Something we have no hold on. Something that belongs only to God. Something that we can only receive. Consider an insight from George MacDonald (1824–1905): "The care of the disciples was care for the day, not for the morrow; the word morrow must

48 Nirmita Panchel, Rabah Kamal, Cynthia Cox, and Rachel Garfield, "The Implications of COVID-19 for Mental Health and Substance Abuse," Kaiser Family Foundation, February 10, 2021, https://www.kff.org/coronavirus-covid-19/issue-brief/the-implications-of-covid-19-for-mental-health-and-substance-use/.

stand for any and every point in the future. The next hour, the next moment, is as much beyond our grasp and as much in God's care, as that a hundred years away. Care for the next minute is just as foolish as care for the morrow, or for a day in the next thousand years—in neither can we do anything, in both God is doing everything. . . . The next [moment] is nowhere till God has made it."[49] The cosmos and you and I with it are reliant upon the providence of God from which each moment, hour, and epoch flow. Discipleship, abiding in the imagination of faith, invites the person to trust in Jesus Christ alone, which in turn values the now for the sake of the now. The present becomes the playground of the imagination of faith.

The pinnacle of the pericope is an unusual command: Consider the lilies of the field, how they grow.[50] That is, pay attention to the ditch daisies, how they grow. The verb Jesus uses here is important: καταμάθετε (*ka-ta-MATH-e-te*). It is an imperative, a command, which in Greek is an aorist, second-person plural, of the verb καταμανθάνω (*ka-ta-man-THAH-o*), which is itself a compound verb rooted in μανθάνω (*man-THAH-o*), meaning I learn or I observe or I comprehend or I wonder, with the prefix κατά serving to amp up the verb just a bit. In short, Jesus says, "Pay attention, y'all."

What can we learn from this word?

Grammatically, the force of the aorist tense upon the imperative mood (or vice versa!) results in a type of "summary command"[51]—more a *way of being* than a process. The audience of Jesus's command is everyone within earshot—disciples, crowd, bystanders. He throws it out there rather willy-nilly. It's out there for all. Such "considering" is not limited. While it is a command, it leans toward being an invitation for all to pay attention, to observe, to ponder. A way of being. The ditch daisies (a.k.a. the lilies of the field) are the stated object of consideration in this text. It is important that the lilies are not something restrictive but a symbol for anything that might be considered.

49 George MacDonald, "The Cause of Spiritual Stupidity," 108, quoted in MacDonald, *George MacDonald*, 39.

50 καταμάθετε τὰ κρίνα τοῦ ἀγροῦ πῶς αὐξάνουσιν (Matt 6:28b).

51 Wallace, *Greek Grammar*, IV.B.1.

A final linguistic, grammatical note: the verb here, a form of καταμανθάνω, is a cognate of μανθάνω, which is the root of μαθητής (*math-ei-TEIS*), or disciple. While it might be bending the semantics of Jesus's imperative just a bit, consider that Jesus is inviting us to rethink what discipleship means. As noted, discipleship is regularly doing-focused, which can and does lead to the cul-de-sac of self-righteous boasting.[52] Perhaps the imitation of Christ that is associated with discipleship is looking upon the world with wonder, inhabiting the imagination of faith, seeing the world as it is in Christ, by whose death God reconciled *all things* to God's self.

IMAGINATION AND FREEDOM

Shackles are real and insidious, whether they be internal or external, social or psychological, made of iron or made of memories. Trusting in Jesus does matter for those in any of these kinds of chains. The imagination of faith reveals the world as it is in Christ, but there are times and circumstances and systems wherein the freedom offered by the imagination of faith is not complete. Even the heart and the mind can be shackled.

Maya Angelou's poem "Caged Bird" envisions two birds: one free and one caged. Both can fly. Both can sing. The nature of the caged bird's song is markedly different, however. Here is the second half of the poem:

---

52 Bonhoeffer's influential work *Discipleship* ends with this reflection: "Since we have been formed in the image of Christ, we can live following his example. On this basis, we are now actually able to do those deeds, and in the simplicity of discipleship, to live life in the likeness of Christ. Here simple obedience to the word takes place. I no longer cast even a single glance on my own life, on the new image I bear. For in the same moment that I would desire to see it, I would lose it. For it is, of course, merely the mirror reflection of the image of Jesus Christ upon which I look without ceasing"; Bonhoeffer, *Discipleship*, in *DBW* 4.287–88.

The free bird thinks of another breeze
and the trade winds soft through the sighing trees
and the fat worms waiting on a dawn bright lawn
and he names the sky his own.

But a caged bird stands on the grave of dreams
his shadow shouts on a nightmare scream
his wings are clipped and his feet are tied
so he opens his throat to sing.

The caged bird sings
with a fearful trill
of things unknown
but longed for still
and his tune is heard
on the distant hill
for the caged bird
sings of freedom.[53]

The song of freedom ringing forth from the cage calls out for what is only accessible by means of imagination. The incongruence of experience and song may well result in a bitter reality. The privilege of freedom relegating the sweetness of freedom to mere white noise inaudible for its regularity.

There is a danger in all this talk of trust, imagination, and freedom. Faith's focus on who God is and who we are in Christ, in spite of our persistent capacity to trust that which is not God, can open life to apathy and quietism. Of this, we must be mindful, trusting the "epistle of straw"[54] to admonish us when need be: "If a brother or sister is naked and lacks daily food and one of you says to them, 'Go in peace; keep warm and eat your fill,' and yet you do not supply their bodily needs, what is the good of that? So faith by itself, if

53 Angelou, *Shaker, Why Don't You Sing?*, 16–17.

54 Luther was not fond of James, calling it an "epistle of straw" because "it has nothing of the nature of the gospel about it"; *LW* 35.362.

it has no works, is dead" (Jas 2:15–17). The admonishment here in James, it seems to me, is about a fairly common failure of imagination. Trusting in Jesus means participating in the life of the crucified and risen Christ and in the lives of the world, the neighbor, and the enemy. Trusting in Jesus does not isolate us from the world; it calls us deeper into the world, into the wacky reality of loving our enemies. The freedom that comes with the imagination of faith is not a permission slip for ignoring the world around us, the shackles of our neighbors, the humanity of our enemies. The freedom that accompanies the imagination of faith opens the door for the Christian, freed from the power of sin and death, to live for the neighbor in all kinds of ways, cooperating with anyone who might care to share. Faith active in love, remembering that Jesus can take whatever we bring and declare it faith, as Paul says. True freedom in Christ invites the Christian to abide with and work alongside anyone, trusting that God is good and that God has defeated the power of sin and death and that God has reconciled *all things* to God's self in Christ, even though we might not as yet have the eyes to see.

The imagination of faith encircles the world and reveals it as it is in Christ Jesus.

Abbreviations

BC	*Book of Concord: The Confessions of the Evangelical Lutheran Church*. Edited by Robert Kolb and Timothy J. Wengert. Minneapolis: Fortress, 2000.
BDAG	Bauer, Walter, F. W. Danker, W. F. Arndt, and F. W. Gingrich, eds. *A Greek-English Lexicon of the New Testament and Other Early Christian Literature*. 3rd ed. Chicago: University of Chicago Press, 2000.
DBW	*Dietrich Bonhoeffer Works*. Edited by Wayne Whitson Floyd Jr. 17 vols. Minneapolis: Fortress, 1998–2014.
LW	*Luther's Works* (American ed.). Edited by Helmut Lehmann and Jaroslav Pelikan. 55 vols. Philadelphia: Fortress / St. Louis: Concordia, 1955–86.
WA	Luther, Martin. *Luthers Werke: Kritische Gesamtausgabe [Schriften]*. 73 vols. Weimar: H. Böhlau, 1883–2009.
WABr	Luther, Martin. *Luthers Werke: Kritische Gesamtausgabe: Briefwechsel*. 18 vols. Weimar: H. Böhlau, 1930–85.

Bibliography

Abraham, Anna. "Surveying the Imagination Landscape." In *The Cambridge Handbook of the Imagination*, edited by Anna Abraham, 1–10. Cambridge: Cambridge University Press, 2020.

Agee, Jennifer. *Systematic Mythology: Imagining the Invisible.* Eugene, OR: Wipf & Stock, 2019.

Ambridge, Ben, and Elena V. M. Lieven. *Child Language Acquisition: Contrasting Theoretical Approaches.* Cambridge: Cambridge University Press, 2011.

Angelou, Maya. *Shaker, Why Don't You Sing?* New York: Random House, 1983.

Aulen, Gustaf. *The Faith of the Christian Church.* Translated by E. H. Wahlstrom and G. E. Arden. Philadelphia: Muhlenberg, 1948.

Barth, Karl. *The Epistle to the Romans.* 6th ed. Translated by Edwyn Hoskyns. London: Oxford University Press, 1968.

Beason, Tyrone. "A Nearly All-White Iowa Town Asked Itself: 'Why Do We Hate?'" *Los Angeles Times*, January 31, 2020. https://www.latimes.com/politics/story/2020-01-31/dubuque-iowa-confronts-racism.

Becker, Ernest. *The Denial of Death.* New York: Free Press, 1973.

Ben-Naim, Arieh. *Entropy Demystified: The Second Law Reduced to Plain Common Sense.* Rev. ed. Hackensack, NJ: World Scientific, 2008.

Bonhoeffer, Dietrich. *Life Together and Prayerbook of the Bible.* Edited by Gerhard Ludwig Müller, Albrecht Schönherr, and Geffrey B. Kelly. Translated by Daniel W. Bloesch and James H. Burtness. Vol. 5. of *Dietrich Bonhoeffer Works.* Minneapolis: Fortress, 1996.

——. *Theological Education at Finkenwalde: 1935–1937.* Edited by Victoria J. Barnett and Barbara Wojhoski. Translated by Douglas W. Stott. Vol. 14 of *Dietrich Bonhoeffer Works*. Minneapolis: Fortress, 2013.

Bonhoeffer, Dietrich, and Clyde E. Fant. *Bonhoeffer: Worldly Preaching.* Nashville: Thomas Nelson, 1975.

Bretherton, Inge. "Attachment Theory: Retrospect and Prospect." *Growing Points of Attachment Theory and Research: Monographs of the Society for Research in Child Development* 50, nos. 1–2 (1985): 3–35.

Buber, Martin. *I and Thou*. Translated by Walter Kaufmann. New York: Charles Scribner's Sons, 1970.

Byrne, Ruth M. J. *The Rational Imagination: How People Create Alternatives to Reality.* Cambridge, MA: MIT Press, 2005.

Calvin, Jean, and Ford Lewis Battles. *Calvin: Institutes of the Christian Religion*. Louisville, KY: Westminster / John Knox, 2001.

Carson, Rachel. *The Sense of Wonder: A Celebration of Nature for Parents and Children*. New York: Harper Perennial, 1956.

Chase, Alston Hurd, and Henry Phillips Jr. *A New Introduction to Greek*. 3rd rev. ed. Cambridge, MA: Harvard University Press, 1961.

Childs, Brevard S. *An Introduction to the Old Testament as Scripture*. Philadelphia: Fortress, 1979.

——. *The Struggle to Understand Isaiah as Christian Scripture.* Grand Rapids, MI: Eerdmans, 2004.

Coggins, Richard, and Jin H. Han. *Six Minor Prophets through the Centuries*. Blackwell Bible Commentary. Oxford: Wiley-Blackwell, 2011.

Davies, Jim. *Imagination: The Science of Your Mind's Greatest Power.* New York: Pegasus, 2019.

Day, Dorothy. *The Long Loneliness*. San Francisco: Harper & Row, 1952.

Descartes, René. *A Discourse on the Method of Correctly Conducting One's Reason and Seeking Truth in the Sciences*. Translated by Ian MacLean. Oxford: Oxford University Press, 2006.

Dines, Jennifer. *The Septuagint*. Edited by Michael A. Knibb. London: T&T Clark, 2004.

Endo, Masanobu. *Creation and Christology*. WUNT 2.149. Tübingen: Mohr Siebeck, 2002.

Erickson, Jonathan. *Imagination in the Western Psyche: From Ancient Greece to Modern Neuroscience*. Research in Analytical Psychology and Jungian Studies. London: Routledge, 2020.

Flieger, Verlyn. *There Would Always Be a Fairy Tale: More Essays on Tolkien*. Kent, OH: Kent State University Press, 2017.

Freeden, Michael. *Ideology: A Very Short Introduction*. Oxford: Oxford University Press, 2003.

Frei, Hans W. *The Eclipse of Biblical Narrative*. New Haven, CT: Yale University Press, 1974.

Fuller, Robert C. *Wonder: From Emotion to Spirituality*. Chapel Hill: University of North Carolina Press, 2006.

Gadamer, Hans-Georg. *Truth and Method*. 2nd rev. ed. Translated by Joel Weinsheimer and Donald G. Marshall. New York: Crossroad, 1990.

Gafney, Wilda C. *Womanist Midrash: A Reintroduction to the Women of the Torah and the Throne*. Louisville, KY: Westminster / John Knox, 2017.

Gerstenberger, Erhard S. *Theologies in the Old Testament*. Translated by John Bowden. London: T&T Clark, 2002.

Giere, S. D. "*Babette's Feast* (1987)." In *Bible and Cinema: 50 Key Films*, edited by Adele Reinhartz, 18–24. London: Routledge, 2013.

———. "The Eighth-Day Kiss of Psalm 85." *Lutheran Forum* 45, no. 4 (Winter 2011): 10–13.

———. "Faith and the Lord's Making-New in the Old Testament." *Lutheran Forum* 55, no. 2 (Summer 2021): 25–30.

———. *A New Glimpse of Day One: Intertextuality, History of Interpretation, and Genesis 1.1–5*. Beihefte zur Zeitschrift für die neutestamentliche Wissenschaft 172. Berlin: de Gruyter, 2009.

———. "Practice of Being Rooted in the Gospel." *Currents in Theology and Mission* 38, no. 5 (2011): 317–321.

Green, Garrett. *Imagining Theology: Encounters with God in Scripture, Interpretation, and Aesthetics*. Grand Rapids, MI: Baker, 2020.

Greene, Graham. *The Power and the Glory*. New York: Open Road, 1940.

Gupta, Nijay. *Paul and the Language of Faith*. Grand Rapids, MI: Eerdmans, 2020.

Hagen Pifer, Jeanette. *Faith as Participation: An Exegetical Study of Some Key Pauline Texts*. Wissenschaftliche Untersuchungen zum Neuen Testament 2.486. Tübingen: Mohr Siebeck, 2019.

Hall, Douglas John. *The Cross in Our Context: Jesus and the Suffering World*. Minneapolis: Fortress, 2003.

Hancock, Angela Dienhart. *Karl Barth's Emergency Homiletic, 1932–1933: A Summons to Prophetic Witness at the Dawn of the Third Reich*. Grand Rapids, MI: Eerdmans, 2013.

Hardin, Russell. *Trust and Trustworthiness*. New York: Russell Sage Foundation, 2002.

Harrington, Daniel J. "Paul's Use of the Old Testament in Romans." *Studies in Christian-Jewish Relations* 4 (2009): CP1–8.

Hart, Trevor. "Through the Arts: Hearing, Seeing and Touching the Truth." In *Beholding the Glory: Incarnation through the Arts*, edited by Jeremy Begbie, 3–26. Grand Rapids, MI: Baker Academic, 2001.

Hauser, Alan J., and Duane F. Watson, eds. *A History of Biblical Interpretation*. 3 vols. Grand Rapids, MI: Eerdmans, 2003–2017.

Hawley, Katherine. *How to Be Trustworthy*. Oxford: Oxford University Press, 2019.

———. *Trust: A Very Short Introduction*. Oxford: Oxford University Press, 2012.

Hendrix, Scott H. *Martin Luther: Visionary Reformer*. New Haven, CT: Yale University Press, 2017.

Hollis, James. *The Archetypal Imagination*. Carolyn and Ernest Fay Series in Analytical Psychology 8. College Station: Texas A&M, 2000.

Hurtado, Larry W. *God in New Testament Theology*. Library of Biblical Theology. Nashville: Abingdon, 2010.

Jewett, Robert. *Romans: A Commentary*. Hermeneia. Minneapolis: Fortress, 2006.

Jobes, Karen, and Moisés Silva. *Invitation to the Septuagint*. 2nd ed. Grand Rapids, MI: Baker, 2015.

Kierkegaard, Søren. *Kierkegaard's Journals and Notebooks*. Vol. 2, *Journals EE–KK*, edited by Niels Jørgen Cappelørn, Alastair Hannay, David Kangas, Bruce H. Kirmmse, Vanessa Rumble, and K. Brian Söderquist. Princeton: Princeton University Press, 2015.

Kind, Amy, and Peter Kung. "The Puzzle of the Imaginative Use." In *Knowledge through Imagination*, edited by Amy Kind and Peter Kung, 1–34. Oxford: Oxford University Press, 2016.

Kolb, Robert, and Timothy W. Wengert, eds. *The Book of Concord*. Minneapolis: Fortress, 2000.

Legaspi, Michael C. *The Death of Scripture and the Rise of Biblical Studies*. Oxford Studies in Historical Theology. Oxford: Oxford University Press, 2010.

Lehrer, Jonah. *Proust Was a Neuroscientist*. Boston: Houghton Mifflin, 2007.

Levenson, Jon. *The Hebrew Bible, the Old Testament, and Historical Criticism: Jews and Christians in Biblical Studies*. Louisville, KY: Westminster / John Knox, 1993.

Lewis, C. S. *A Grief Observed*. New York: HarperCollins, 1989.

Liddell, Henry George, and Robert Scott. *A Greek-English Lexicon*. Rev. and augmented. Oxford: Clarendon, 1996.

Lightman, Alan. *A Sense of the Mysterious: Science and the Human Spirit*. New York: Pantheon, 2005.

Lindbeck, George. *The Nature of Doctrine: Reason and Theology in a Postliberal Age*. Louisville, KY: Westminster / John Knox, 1984.

Luther, Martin. *Reading the Psalms with Luther: The Psalter for Individual and Family Devotions*. Translated by Bruce A. Cameron. Saint Louis, MO: Concordia, 1993.

MacDonald, George. *George MacDonald: An Anthology 365 Readings*. Edited by C. S. Lewis. San Francisco: HarperCollins, 1946.

——. *Phantastes: A Faerie Romance*. Garden City, NY: Dover, 2005.

——. *Unspoken Sermons: Series I, II, III—Complete and Unabridged*. Great Britain, 2016.

MacGuire, Anne. "Gnosis and Nag Hammadi." In *The Routledge Companion to Early Christian Thought*, edited by D. Jeffery Bingham, 204–226. London: Routledge, 2010.

Mannermaa, Tuomo. *Christ Present in Faith: Luther's View of Justification*. Edited by Kirsi Stjerna. Minneapolis: Fortress, 2005.

McFarland, Ian A. *The Word Made Flesh: A Theology of the Incarnation*. Louisville, KY: Westminster / John Knox, 2019.

McIntyre, Lee. *Post-truth*. The MIT Press Essential Knowledge Series. Cambridge, MA: MIT Press, 2018.

Modell, Arnold H. *Imagination and the Meaningful Brain*. Cambridge, MA: MIT Press, 2003.

Morgan, Teresa. *Roman Faith and Christian Faith: Pistis and Fides in Early Roman Empire and the Early Churches*. Oxford: Oxford University Press, 2015.

Mosser, Carl. "Recovering the Reformation's Ecumenical Vision of Redemption as Deification and Beatific Vision." *Perichoresis* 18, no. 1 (2020): 3–24.

Murphy, G. Ronald, SJ. *Tree of Salvation: Yggdrasil and the Cross of the North*. Oxford: Oxford University Press, 2013.

Oberman, Heiko A. *Luther: Man between God and the Devil*. Translated by Eileen Walliser-Schwarzbart. New York: Image Books, 1989.

——. *The Roots of Anti-Semitism: In the Age of Renaissance and Reformation*. Philadelphia: Fortress, 1984.

Ochs, Peter. "An Introduction to Postcritical Scriptural Interpretation." In *The Return to Scripture in Judaism and Christianity: Essays in Postcritical Scriptural Interpretation*, edited by Peter Ochs, 3–51. Eugene, OR: Wipf & Stock, 1993.

Olds, David L. "The Nurse-Family Partnership: Foundations in Attachment Theory and Epidemiology." In *Enhancing Early Attachments: Theory, Research, Intervention, and Policy*, edited by Lisa J. Berlin, Yair Ziv, Lisa Amaya-Jackson, and Mark T. Greenberg, 217–249. New York: Guilford, 2005.

Orwell, George. *1984*. New York: Berkley, 1949.

Otto, Rudolf. *Idea of the Holy*. 2nd ed. Translated by John W. Harvey. London: Oxford, 1950.

Pelikan, Jaroslav. *The Christian Tradition: A History of the Development of Doctrine*. 5 vols. Chicago: University of Chicago Press, 1971–1991.

Pierce Casey, Robert. *The "Excerpta ex Theodoto" of Clement of Alexandria*. London: Christophers, 1934.

Plass, Ewald M., ed. *What Luther Says: An Anthology*. 3 vols. St. Louis: Concordia, 1959.

Prenter, Regin. *Spiritus Creator*. Translated by John M. Jensen. Philadelphia: Fortress, 1953.

Rae, Murray A. *History and Hermeneutics*. London: T&T Clark, 2005.

Rahlfs, Alfred, comp. *Septuaginta*. Rev. ed. Stuttgart: Deutsche Bibbelgesellschaft, 2006.

Reid, Barbara E. *Wisdom's Feast: An Invitation to Feminist Interpretation of the Scriptures*. Grand Rapids, MI: Eerdmans, 2016.

Ricoeur, Paul. *Interpretation Theory: Discourse and the Surplus of Meaning*. Fort Worth: Texas Christian University Press, 1976.

Ridderbos, Herman N. *Paul: An Outline of His Theology*. Grand Rapids, MI: Eerdmans, 1975.

Rizzolatti, Giacomo, and Michael A. Arbib. "Language within Our Grasp." *Trends in Neuroscience* 21, no. 5 (May 1998): 188–194.

Rovelli, Carlo. *The Order of Time*. Translated by Erica Segre and Simon Carnell. New York: Riverhead, 2018.

Russell, Bertrand. *History of Western Philosophy*. 1946. Reprint, London: Routledge Classics, 2004.

Scheman, Naomi. "Trust and Trustworthiness." In Simon, *Routledge Handbook of Trust*, 28–40.

Seitz, Christopher. *Word without End: The Old Testament as Abiding Theological Witness*. Waco, TX: Baylor University Press, 2004.

Simard, Suzanne W., Kevin J. Beiler, Marcus A. Bingham, Julie R. Deslippe, Leanne J. Philip, and François P. Teste. "Mycorrhizal

Networks: Mechanisms, Ecology and Modelling." *Fungal Biology Review* 26, no. 1 (April 2012): 39–60.

Simon, Judith, ed. *The Routledge Handbook of Trust and Philosophy.* New York: Routledge, 2020.

Smith, Christian, and Melissa Lundquist Denton. *Soul Searching: The Religious and Spiritual Lives of American Teenagers.* Oxford: Oxford University Press, 2005.

Soulen, Richard N., and R. Kendall Soulen. *Handbook of Biblical Criticism.* 4th ed. Louisville, KY: Westminster / John Knox, 2011.

Steigmann-Gall, Richard. *The Holy Reich: Nazi Conceptions of Christianity, 1919–1945.* Cambridge: Cambridge University Press, 2004.

Steinmetz, David C. "The Superiority of Pre-critical Exegesis." *Theology Today* 37, no. 1 (1980): 27–38.

Stråth, Bo. "Ideology and Conceptual History." In *The Oxford Handbook of Political Ideologies*, edited by Michael Freeden, Lyman Tower Sargent, and Marc Stears, 3–19. Oxford: Oxford University Press, 2013.

Stuempfle, Herman. *Preaching Law and Gospel.* Ramsey, NJ: Sigler, 1990.

Sugirtharah, R. S. *The Bible and Asia: From the Pre-Christian Era to the Postcolonial Age.* Cambridge, MA: Harvard University Press, 2013.

Tillich, Paul. "He Who Is the Christ." In *The Shaking of the Foundations*, 141–148. New York: Charles Scribner's Sons, 1948.

Tolkien, J. R. R. "On Fairy Stories." In *Tree and Leaf*, 1–82. 1964. Reprint, London: HarperCollins, 1988.

Tracy, David. *Plurality and Ambiguity: Hermeneutics, Religion, Hope.* Chicago: University of Chicago Press, 1987.

Trible, Phyllis. *Texts of Terror: Literary-Feminist Readings of Biblical Narratives.* Overtures to Biblical Theology. Philadelphia: Fortress, 1984.

Viereck, George Sylvester. "What Life Means to Einstein." *Saturday Evening Post*, October 26, 1929.

Wallace, Daniel B. *Greek Grammar beyond the Basics: An Exegetical Syntax of the New Testament.* Grand Rapids, MI: Zondervan, 1996.

Warnock, Mary. *Imagination*. London: Faber and Faber, 1976.
Wingren, Gustaf. *The Living Word: A Theological Study of Preaching and the Church*. Translated by Victor C. Pogue. Eugene, OR: Wipf & Stock, 1960.
Yarchin, William. *History of Biblical Interpretation: A Reader*. Grand Rapids, MI: Baker Academic, 2004.
Yee, Gale A. *The Hebrew Bible: Feminist and Intersectional Perspectives*. Minneapolis: Fortress, 2018.
Žižek, Slavoj. *The Sublime Object of Ideology*. London: Verso, 1989.

Ingram Content Group UK Ltd.
Milton Keynes UK
UKHW010725190423
420414UK00005B/591